SUPERNATURAL HOMECOMINGS

SUPERNATURAL HOMECOMINGS

MOFFAT DAVID

MiReads

A word of thanks

I would like to say thanks to the following people for their tremendous help in this supernatural book.

Dad and mum, uncles John and Ezekiel (my dad's elder brother and my elder dad's according to our Malawian culture) for the stories from our home village.

Pastor David Kalilani, Pastor Frank Gondwe, Pr. McDonald Mkandawire, Mizeck Chiweza, Faith, Triphonia. Aunt Agness Kalawe, Ruth Banda, Mrs. Lungu and Mr. Wells Sakala, for the personal and insightful testimonies.

Yamiko Yakobe, what a beautiful and vibrant cover design.

Pr. Zenzo of Impact Church USA. You are a true brother and a real blessing.... and continue being one, May God expand your territory! Thank you for your kind introduction.

What story will you read?

Contents

Sean and Aretha
"You inspire and energize me"

Debbie
"You are forever cherished"

Dad and Danielle
"I miss you"

Foreword

I'm a fairly new pastor. My wife Michelle and I launched Impact Church in 2015. As you can imagine, pastoring is filled with so many amazing joys, but it also has its challenges. The most challenging thing I have to do in my role as pastor is conduct funerals.

You should have seen how terrified I was when I was asked to preach at the cemetery before burying one of the mothers in our church. I could not sleep the night before. I kept saying to Michelle, "This is so difficult." I dreaded it and didn't want to do it, but, of course, I had to. I'm the pastor! That's when I first realized how difficult the pastor's task of helping families cope with life after loss is. That's also when I realized that we don't have enough resources for helping people deal with death. God does not want us to be ignorant when it comes to this very important matter.

"Now we do not want you to be uninformed, believers, about those who are asleep [in death], so that you will not grieve [for them] as the others do who have no hope [beyond this present life]. For if we believe that Jesus died and rose again [as in fact He did], even so God [in this same way—by raising them from the dead] will bring with Him those [believers] who have fallen asleep in Jesus." 1 Thessalonians 4:13-14 (AMP).

That's why I am so excited about this book that my dear, longtime friend and brother Moffat has written. This book is critical and much needed for our generation. This is a manual that lays a blueprint for everyone. Whether it's for those who are grieving the loss of loved ones, for friends of those who are in the grieving process, or pastors, leaders, or bosses of those grieving, this is a book that will help you prepare for how to deal with death. We all have to deal with death at some point in life.

That's something no one on earth can escape. Just as it says in Hebrews 9:27 that

"And as it is appointed for men to die once, but after this the judgment." (NKJV)

I also conducted a funeral after a member from my church lost her mother. She lost her father first, then her mom, all in a matter of two months. Another pastor did her father's funeral, but I did her mother's. Though both parents were believers when they died, this church member anticipated her mother's funeral to be harder to deal with (especially at the cemetery) than her father's. Yet, she told me that she felt more comforted during her mother's funeral than at her father's because of the revelation I shared during my message.

She said that the pastor who did her father's funeral actually made it more painful for her. He kept emphasizing how her father was being buried into the ground. What a rough image to have - that the person you love is being buried in the earth as their final destination. On the contrary, I kept emphasizing how her mother was not in the ground but in heaven with Jesus, walking on streets of gold. I told her that we were just returning the "container" (the body) that carried her while on the earth back into the ground and that her mother was already in heaven. My focus was on heaven where her spirit truly was, not the ground where her body was. For a believer, this is the comforting truth. She was saved!

"For this we say to you by the word of the Lord, that we who are alive and remain until the coming of the Lord will by no means precede those who are asleep. For the Lord Himself will descend from heaven with a shout, with the voice of an archangel, and with the trumpet of God. And the dead in Christ will rise first. Then we who are alive and remain shall be caught up together with them in the clouds to meet the Lord in the air. And thus we shall always be with the Lord. Therefore, comfort one another with these words." 1 Thessalonians 4:15-18 (NKJV)

The right revelation about death, or life after death, brings understanding and great comfort. I believe with everything in me that this book will do just that for you as you read it. It will bring comfort, clarity to unanswered questions, and a focus on the real truth about death. And to those who have not secured the ticket to heaven as your final destination, don't worry, there is a prayer at the end of this book that will help you to do just that. If you pray that simple salvation prayer, you will be saved and go through this life knowing that you have a beautiful destination after this life. Heaven is a beautiful place. There is no sorrow. No more tears. Only joy and peace forever more!

"And I heard a loud voice from the throne saying, "Look! God's dwelling place is now

among the people, and he will dwell with them. They will be his people, and God himself will be with them and be their God.

'He will wipe every tear from their eyes. There will be no more death' or mourning or crying or pain, for the old order of things has passed away." Revelation 21:3-4 (NIV)

"But those who die in the Lord will live; their bodies will rise again!

Those who sleep in the earth will rise up and sing for joy!

For your life-giving light will fall like dew on your people in the place of the dead!" Isaiah 26:19 (NLT)

Pastor Zenzo Matoga
Senior Pastor, Impact Church

Introduction

This is the second edition of my book, and before writing my first book I had never written, imagined I would write, nor had I seen many books quite like this one. I had heard stories of near death experiences but heard few from a practical and experiential Christian perspective.

Supernatural homecomings is a book that unlocks the mystery of how we all pass on to the next life and die to this life. It's based on real life accounts of circumstances surrounding the demise of mostly Christians, their experiences which involved seeing the divine and the "spiritual world" manifest in this present and "physical world" just as they passed on!

This book is not a book of fairy tales, it is based on real life experiences! A fair share of them are of people I know and an even larger share are of my very own relatives. Especially in this second edition, more of such have been added.

You may have lost someone close to you and wondered where they are. I share the feeling... after losing my only sister, and later a spouse and a father, I initially wondered just like everyone else, what really happens when we die? Where do these loved ones go? And is there hope?

Well the answers will blow you away! You might just discover that there is a world out there that is, perhaps, more real than our own and, in fact, that is more permanent than our own. Most of all, this book is an encouragement that there is a grander purpose that God has for you and I, the purpose is that we would eventually go home to our Father and receive a grate reward for our love and obedience to him on this earth. What's even more amazing, is how graciously our Father reaches out to us and takes us home when it's our time to depart.

Therefore our prayer should be for God to "teach us to number our days" so we may live lives of meaning and purpose on this earth.

I am not hoping that you will be amused or startled at the amazing stories herein, though startled you will be! I am hoping more that you will be encouraged... That perhaps the tears you shed may be wiped away by God. Not that you will forget or diminish the absence of your loved one but that you will be filled with hope and strength for things to come as you remember them. Because remember them you will, and that, continuously. And, because time does not heal... only God does.

But ultimately, that you may find your way to your very own father, by connecting with him and finding the door to heaven who is Jesus Christ! If you have him, you have your ticket to the pearly gates of our heavenly home! I am hoping that perhaps there would be a spark in your eyes and that a fire would be stoked in your heart, that you will eagerly yearn for your heavenly home.

Not now, but only when your time comes, that you too may see visions of heaven! That you too may one day say, "I have a father, and I have a heavenly home!" infinitely better and infinitely more beautiful than your current home no matter how humble or lavish, your current home may be!

So..... be encouraged! And be blessed as you read these amazing stories!!

Moffat David

Tonia

Comforted by Jesus himself

Tonia lost her dad when she was only a child. She never really had the chance to know him and was raised by her mum alone. She had now grown into a young lady and was finishing her high school. Fortunately, she went to college and graduated. When she looked back at her life she could only attribute this to God's grace. And at least she had her mom who helped take care of her.

In college, as she was about to graduate, she came to know God much deeper and received Jesus as Lord and savior. She felt a sense of peace and purpose and came to the realization that this was the Jesus who had provided for their family all through her life in the absence of her father. He was and had been, in essence, their father and defense.

As soon as she graduated, however, tragedy struck. She lost her mother after a short illness... Her pillar, and her rock had gone, and she was left all alone. No one to provide for her, to love her and encourage her in the way only a mother could.

The road ahead was torturous... emotionally torturous. She had just come to know Jesus and was literally a babe in the faith. Her new found faith gave her an expectation of the Lord's blessings and the best in life, but here she was, her tender heart torn apart and totally devastated! Once again!

'Why her?' She thought, oooh don't we all think that? Where was God when this was happening? Why now? When she was not even settled in life and had not even found a job?

She searched for answers but could not find them. She listened to and sat in numerous sermons but they were not directed at her pain. No one could understand the void in her heart, nor could anyone settle the storm of chaos and confusion that raged in her fragile mind! She was stunned and totally broken.

She lived like this for a year, still praying and still clinging on to God. One thing she knew was that she couldn't let go of God. She couldn't give up on him. She didn't get all the answers to her questions but she somehow felt that if she lets go of God who else can she hold on to? Anything or anyone else was as limited as she was and all she could do was hold on. And hold she did. She held on through the darkness, and held on through pain. All through the confusion, and all through the despair. It all seemed dark and dreary... but she held on!

Still confused and sad, still full of questions, and now one year on, she had a dream. This dream was like no other. She was taken to a lovely and divine place, bright and shiny, with streets of gold and she just knew it was heaven.

She saw her mother who had passed on a year ago. Her mum was sitting close to Jesus, and talking with him. She just observed them from a distance, she observed the joy, the peace and love they shared! It was so precious and enviable. Enviable in the holiest sense of the word of course! If ever envy can be holy!

Then her mother saw her standing at a distance and came towards her. Her mother spoke to her and told her about the day she died. She said there was a celebration in heaven, there was rejoicing at her homecoming. A trumpet was blown announcing her arrival and all heaven was filled with joy.

She realized that she had never thought of her mother's death in this way. Indeed to her, it was a death on earth but in heaven it was a birth of something new. It was a homecoming and a day when the hopes of every Christian are fulfilled! The promise of eternal life became a reality to her mother and this is what would await her too if she holds on to her faith in Jesus. Her own death would be a transition from one life to the next a homecoming filled with joy and celebration.

Shortly, a young man came along and started talking with Jesus, he looked at Tonia and asked Jesus

"Who is this young lady?"

"That's Tonia, your daughter"

Tonia could not believe this was her Dad, he looked so young and energetic and with no signs of old age at all'

"She's all grown up now and she has turned out to be a lovely young lady under your care. Is it her time to come home?'

'No, no, no, it's not yet time for her' Jesus said,

"Its just that she has been so distraught over the past year due to the passing of her mom and I wanted to show her heaven so she can be comforted. Now she will know that she should not worry about you. She will know that you are both in my care and that she too is in my care right there on earth. I have been a father to her in your absence until now and will continue to care for her. She will have the joy and hope of heaven and know that all is well.'

After Jesus said these words, she woke up. And wondered what manner of dream this was. As soon as the day broke, she got ready and rushed to her friend Ruth and told her the dream.

'This is what I dreamt' she said.

"I have so much peace. I was so desperately distraught but not anymore. I had no peace at all and sometimes I could cry through the night. Whenever I remembered my mother I would become a teary mess, I would be overcome with self-pity and depression and have no hope for the future. But now, even though I miss my mom I know she is in God's care, I know she is safe and above all, I know she is home! And.... and... I will meet her one day. I will meet her one day and be united forever'.

Ruth was amazed at the dream. She had stood with Tonia in her ups and downs. She knew Tonia was having a tough time as a new believer in Jesus Christ. She knew she had unanswered questions and that she was overcome with sorrow.

All she could do for her during this time was pray for her. And pray she did. Passionately, lovingly and committedly. Having experienced loss herself she knew the pain that Tonia felt. Ruth herself had lost her own mom a few years back. She was only left with her sister Patience. The two of them had to stand together, they were 'each other's mommies' and stood together in thick and thin. They stood together in prayer and helped each other out in the home. They prayed together and encouraged one other. But...barely a year and some months later her only sister and remaining sibling also passed. She too was in pain about the same time that Tonia was experiencing her own pain. But though in pain her faith was a little more rooted and she knew that despite the pain there is the hope of eternal life.

When Tonia told her the dream she had, Ruth was happy and excited on several fronts. First, that her dear friend was encouraged and comforted by such a divine encounter and revelation of heaven. She was hopeful that Tonia's faith won't be shattered. Secondly, she saw this as her own answered prayer, she had been praying for Tonia over the past year and this is how God came through for her! What an amazing answer to desperate prayer!

But someone else was encouraged. She was encouraged! Here she was, worried more about her friend when she too felt the same pain. The dream and vision she was given also encouraged her! She was comforted by what she heard and also thought of her own mother and sibling sister'.

'All is not lost' she thought

'I will see them again, I will see them again'

'Thank you Jesus for eternal life' she prayed, "thank you Jesus for such a precious gift.

2

Ayaya

And his heavenly orchestra

Ayaya is quite a reverent name. It's one of the several words used for granny or grandpa by children and grandchildren, words like 'anganga' and 'agogo', even words like 'mbuya' they all mean the same thing. It's not only grandpa or grandma depicting their age, no, it also implies, the wise one, or the experienced one. It's a reverent name but also a deeply intimate one. It's a name that shows deep pride, literally celebrating the life of the elderly and the gift of readily available wisdom they are to the family. Wisdom that is cherished, when children need that unique guidance, that only a grand parent can bring, wisdom and love that is unconditional and uncommon.

For most grandchildren however, it's a name that makes them reminiscent of the free reign they get from their grandparents who rarely discipline them as sternly as their own parents... if at all. This is what they enjoy most, and is the main thing they like about visiting and staying with Ayaya.

If it were a wrestling match we would have said it's a 'no rules' and "no holds barred" game. Kids not only normally jump up and down on the sofa, play outside till sundown, and when they finally come indoors.

they also play till late in the night. No curfew just fun and games... playing tag, hide and seek, pillow fights, follow the leader, tchoo tchoo train ....the works! Going to see Ayaya is heaven on earth for kids and so it was for my aunt Agnes.

She would go and visit her Ayaya with her parents especially at the holidays. His love was unconditional as all grandparents are.... as they would visit him they would set off to a place called Chinkhoma, and right in the village they would be welcomed by a Presbyterian church which was almost in the Centre of the village... And houses mushroomed all around it. In fact, Sunday's were easy for Ayaya as they barely had to walk more than several dozen meters before entering the church doors. As soon as they heard the church bells chiming, they would simply pick up the Bible and be happily seated in church within just a few minutes. What a privilege it was for them. Talk of 'church with benefits' hey!

Aunt Agnes fondly remembers that 'he would occupy his lazy chair on the veranda as he enjoyed his afternoon naps. Perhaps not restricted to the afternoon alone of course....' as she told the story, we laughed at his interesting 'eating and napping routine'.

But this particular holiday Ayaya was not too well. It was clear that age was catching up with him. He would often fall ill as he grew weaker with time and his health would be "on and off". Sometimes feeling better and stronger, while on other occasions he would be weaker and more poorly.

One morning he asked,

'what day is it? Is it Sunday today?'

'No Ayaya it's Wednesday today' they responded

'But it must be Sunday' he insisted.

'But Ayaya it's Wednesday why do you say it's Sunday?

'It's surely Sunday because I can hear singing coming from the church'

'But there is no one in church Ayaya! The church is closed and nothing is happening there!'

'But I hear a choir singing moving towards us'

The family looked at each other and thought,

'It must be the illness, he is starting to imagine things. He needs his rest' they said. Then within a few minutes he started again,

'The choir is now close by, they are near the house, I can hear them going around the house to the main door.'

People in the house looked out the windows and saw no one. They sent for someone to go outside and check who was there but there was no one, just the birds chirping, and the sheep bleating and the cows mooing.

'They are now at the door' he said

Puzzled they continued to look at each other and wonder why Ayaya was saying all this. He did not look delirious or restless as if anything was worse than usual. He was not failing to compose or express himself all morning and there was nothing out of the ordinary, and as far as his illness was concerned, he was rather stable, as stable as any other day.

'Look the choir is here and they have set up a ladder into heaven!' (now in the rural areas ladder means staircase as in the story of "Jacobs ladder" in the Bible)

'They are calling me,

'they say it's time to go'...

'It's time to go now, it's time to go!'

When Ayaya said this, he lay down on his sofa and slept.

After a few minutes the family became curious at what he said just before he lay his head down, they came over and checked his vitals, but saw neither chest movement nor any breathing. He seemed soundly asleep but discovered that, actually, Ayaya was not breathing. Checking his pulse they felt no heart beat and slowly his body grew cold.

'He is gone' the elders among them said, 'He is gone'. They all marveled at how he could die "just like that". Dying in response to an invitation by a heavenly orchestra, an invitation to climb the ladders that they only heard about in the biblical story of Jacob. An invitation to follow a choir that only Ayaya could see and only he could respond to. Aunt Agnes fondly remembers her Ayaya, and as she explained, said that, 'I did not have much time with him since he died when I was quite a young girl. But his departure inspires me till this very day. God sent for him and he departed knowing where his was going and above all, he departed in songs of a heavenly and angelic orchestra'.

3

❧

Triphonia

The girl who had nothing to show for her life

Mangochi is a nice and serene district a place where you can take a relaxing holiday at the lake. It has those spots that you can literally call heaven on earth! Its from this beautiful place that something remarkable happened. Let's listen to Triphonia tell her own story, in her own words.

"In October of 2019, and, on a Saturday morning I was feeling quite ok, and the day was coming along as well as one would ever hope. Chatting away with my friends with everything ok. I literally expected a perfect day.

Then, all of a sudden, as if my expectations jinxed the day, I blacked out. Just like that! And I didn't even know what went wrong till now. Nothing made sense, everything went dark around me. It was a strange feeling of dead silence within me even though I could hear voices of the people around me. But I really couldn't tell what was going on. I could not tell where I was or what was happening to me. This dead silence continued for hours!

For some reason I started feeling like I'm stuck, I couldn't make heads or tails of the feeling or anything around me and it felt as if I was in a box or something like that. I started shouting but it was as if I was shouting from a box. And no matter how much I called, pushed, shoved or stretched nothing was really happening. I felt like no matter how much I shouted there was a gap and distance between me, everyone, and everything else... so I called on the Lord... and for some reason I heard someone call my name, and could then feel the presence of people around me. I could feel that I am no longer in a void and could feel my body again and 'I breathed life'. And someone said 'oh Triphonia you're awake'.

Then they told me that it was around 10pm, and I yet had collapsed at about 1 pm early that afternoon.

After medical examination no diagnosis was given, and they said I seemed perfectly fine. And, as all doctors do, when they are clueless and don't want to show it, they advised me that I was probably under a lot of stress. And of course mark the words 'probably'. But surprisingly they also said they can't detect signs of stress.

My second brush with death was in February of 2020. I was with Peace, my sister. I went to town with her to have my phone repaired. But I was feeling strange. I actually felt a cold chill go over my body. I wasn't physically sick but all I can say is that I felt 'strange' because it was such a bright sunny day for me to feel that cold. This was not really a physical coldness it felt more like it was from within me as opposed to coming from the elements around me. Confused with how I felt I told Peace that,

'I'm not feeling ok. Maybe I should sit down'

But sitting down didn't help, I stood up again but standing up wasn't any better either. The strange feeling just wouldn't go away. All of a sudden, everything went pitch black. But that coldness, oh that coldness! It continued and intensified. I felt it rising from my feet to the rest of my body until I felt that it had now filled my whole body and my whole body went dead cold. At this point I literally stopped feeling my body. But, I was conscious because I heard my sister calling for help and someone holding my body and saying,

'She's getting cold please hurry we need to rush her to the hospital'.

I heard everything around me, I understood what they were saying but much as I wanted to respond I could not. As my confusion increased, immediately I started levitating and rising from my body. I saw my sister, together with another person, holding my body and I could see the tops of cars and then the tops of buildings. Strangely I could see everyone and feel everything.

Then I saw a being in a robe that I can only describe as an angel. I did not see the face, I only saw the back because he was leading me. I wanted to grab the robe but I stopped myself,

'This is stranger danger' I thought,

'This being came from nowhere, passing in front of me and leading me... and I am having the urge to touch his robe.....'

Then it hit me! I might be dying here, and if I grab his robe he'll take me and I'll be gone for good.

'I can't go with this person now' I thought. I then prayed to God and said,

'God if you're taking me, surely it can't be now, and surely it can't be here! Because I haven't achieved my purpose in life, when I look back at my life, I just don't see it, I feel there is nothing I can show for it, and I can't say 'this is what I have done and achieved for you God in my life''.

I felt empty, cheated and let down, and that there was so much more to life. There were some promises that God had given to me and there must be a purpose for my life other than just living and dying on that day. I felt my life had no meaning. So I prayed and cried out to God... I said,

'Lord give me another chance, let me have something to show for my life! Let me do something for you and achieve something with my life, the word of God says, 'we shall live and testify of the goodness of the Lord,' and I have not yet come to a point where I can say I have done something for you and your eternal purposes, I have nothing to testify for you God, so please God! Please! Please give me another chance,'

Now, previously I felt darkness all around me... But this time...it was light, light all around me. The light shone on my chest and from that light came a force on my chest, a really really, really strong force.

Then I started hearing voices of people around me. They told me to respond in any way I could, either to pain or the sounds around me but I could not speak or move. My heart was now beating and my body was getting warmer, I realized a familiar voice of a Dr. from our church. They said I was stable and getting better. They were all perplexed at what happened because their medical tests and attempts to diagnose me did not show anything wrong. But, I knew what had happened to me. Even the nurse on duty that day said he had finished his shift and was going home but when he saw me being rolled into the hospital he felt an urge to help and said to himself, 'let me go and assist this person'. He was beside me throughout until I started talking in the evening. But I was, again, told there was nothing the doctors could diagnose, this nurse turned to me and said,

'Only you know what really happened, because I was the one who looked after you the whole time and I took the tests, and what has happened to you for you to come back to life doesn't make sense or usually happen, your we're dead. I was trying so hard to massage your legs which are usually the first to lose life, I massaged them in order for you to gain sensation and feel your body. I did this continuously the whole time to see if there are returning signs of life. I also don't know what I was doing here in this side of hospital, because this is not even my department, I was just passing through this side of the hospital on my way home, I don't even know why I passed through this side of the hospital because it's not my even usual route when leaving the hospital, that's when I saw you and I just felt I had to help you'.

Surprisingly, I was taken into the emergency room but there were no medical personnel working in the emergency department at all. My sister said 'I don't know what death is but you died in my arms Triphonia, you were dead and you were cold. I prayed that God would spare your life coz this would scar my life. You were completely lifeless in my arms'.

I have heard these stories, of people saying they went to heaven but

I know I died that day. But, I prayed and said 'I need another chance to do something for God and to serve him.'

When I came back, I was completely changed, because sometimes we take life for granted. Life is fragile and can be lost in the blink of an eye. One moment you're alive and the next moment you're dead. And, you have no control over the process, you're completely powerless. In my case, I could see what was happening around me, people who came and tried to help and people who simply avoided me and passed by. It was as if I was also a bystander watching from a distance. But in the midst of the chaos, there was nothing I could do, there was just an overwhelming sense of calm.

Funny enough, before all this happened, the previous day I was continually reminded of the word of God that came to King Hezekiah telling him to keep his house in order.

"About that time Hezekiah became deathly ill, and the prophet Isaiah son of Amoz went to visit him. He gave the king this message: "This is what the Lord says: Set your affairs in order, for you are going to die. You will not recover from this illness."" 2 Kings 20:1 NLT

It kept coming in my mind until late in the night. I wondered why this word kept coming to me and deep in the night I woke up and pondered on what I ought to do with this verse. Should I ask for 15 more years? I felt an urge to call all my sisters and tell them how much I loved and appreciated them. And this I did! One of my sisters got a text message from me and she responded by asking 'why are you talking like that? Are you going somewhere?'

There were some other peculiar events because my 'cold feeling' started at home and my sister, Peace, repeatedly asked me if I was ok and if I really needed to get the phone repaired in town, or it could wait. But I said "yes I'm ok". But even when I was with Peace, I was feeling so much discomfort. Actually my body was boring and sickening me and I felt like it was heavy and weighing me down. In fact, I felt like I wanted to leave it and really couldn't stand it. I could not explain the feeling fully so I could only tell Peace that I am not feeling good.

She said what do you mean you're not feeling good? Do you have any pains or aches or fever or nausea?

'I don't know I'm just not feeling good' I said, there was just was no way of explaining it.

We tried to a couple of things to bring my mojo back but nothing worked. We tried to get some nice food like we usually do, but I had no interest in anything we tried to do. But when this happened to me, I remembered Hezekiah's prayer and I said 'I won't pray for years but only for another chance' that's why I got the boldness to pray. And two weeks later when I was in church, our pastor called me out in church and said

'God has something for you, don't ask questions, of why it happened but one day you will realize what has happened' that's when I knew that God has really given me a purpose and a second chance in life and I could now live my life for God. Remarkably, I did not even tell the pastor what had happened but the word of encouragement came as if he knew exactly what I had gone through and how confusing the whole experience had been to me.

This experience has had a profound impact on my life. We usually think that as Christians we are ok and we don't need anything more than just this 'title'. I received Christ at an early age in secondary school and I got to a place where I was living a life of good 'Christian reputation' and was an example of a godly youth who was even 'shown off' to others by my parents and teachers. I felt that was enough simply because 'I am a Christian and I go to church and do good things'. I thought I don't need to be completely sold-out to God and believed I could afford to have a 'casual faith'.

But in this moment I realized that life is really meaningless when we are living it on our own. I now wanted to live more, and discovered that it's not about having reputation, no! It's about purpose! In fact I previously struggled with my purpose in life. The more confused I got about my purpose the more I lost my 'zest' for life.

I really hated my life, and everything about living, but in that moment I wanted to live more, and now I want to live a long life. I want to do something productive, I want to be effective and a person of influence and to bring positive change to others, not just that I lived on earth and experienced all the pleasures of life. But, I should be able to say 'at least my life meant something to someone, I lived as an example and my life preached to them without me talking to them and I reached out to someone and was a blessing to their life'.

Previously, I did not value life and what death really means. I felt that death is death and it comes to everyone and people die every day. Back in the day, I actually feared death, I would wake up thinking I will die today. But I now realized that life is about "who are you living for?" Now there is more to my life than just living aimlessly each and every day.

I also realized that dying is not dying, because we have always misunderstood the concept of death and its finality, but know I know that death is not just about dying, because in death there is a reward. Previously I thought you simply die like any other living thing, but when we die we get a reward for living and achieving things for God in this life and when I realized that I had nothing to show for, and had no reward for my life, I had to ask for a second chance.

Dying is not dying also because, I discovered that the spirit is always alive. I know some people say people hallucinate or dream, but in my experience, there was nothing of that sort. I was fully conscious all the time I knew that this body of mine is gone. I could see everything happening around me, but I could not feel anything of this earth, not even the air. I know that this body is just a container for our spirit. And I think that, as a believer, there is grace even in death. I can't wait to serve God and live my purpose.

I look forward to living and to living for God.

4

Thokozani

Saved by a mother's teary prayers

Thokozani (meaning 'praise') was a very fond cousin of mine. In our childhood days we used to visit our grandparents together, and spending the holidays there together. By that, I mean we would spend our holidays in the village. Oh yes! The village, with no electricity and no tap water. Our light would come from a lamp, actually the lamp would only be for the living room while the other rooms would use what is called a 'koloboyi'.

A koloboyi is made from a glass or metal jar with a metal lid. You punch a hole in the lid, and through the nail-sized hole you squeeze through a twisted piece of cloth that protrudes from the base of the jar or tin and stays intact without falling down because of a small knot that holds it into place just after its head protrudes from inside the tin.

Once secured, you fill the tin with paraffin (kerosene) and light the knotty tip, it's smoky but effective and very good for lighting the rest of the house without investing in several expensive brand new lamps, quite ideal for a large African family with many kids and grandkids, with no electricity and a slim budget. Perfect African survival and financial management skills. Our water? A well that was situated in the middle of the homestead. It was good for all uses, drinking, cooking and household chores. We were sorted in the village, no bills, no bills, and no bills.

We would play till late into the night playing tag and causing mischief under the full moon and clear night sky. In the mornings we would go hunting for birds and rabbits with our dogs, and be elated when we come home with a rabbit or some birds. And we would go swimming in the nearby river, splashing the cold water on each other's faces. He taught me how to use a sling, not just use, but make it from raw sisal, just as he taught me how to make rope. We would cut the sisal and take a hoe's blade, sticking it upside down into the ground. Then we would scrape off the flesh of the sisal by pulling it across the sharp perpendicular hoe blade to get rid of the fluids and flesh and would remain with only the fiber. The fiber would be rolled and twisted, on our thighs! And three of these strands would be taken to be woven into a tough rope. As if that was not enough adventure, finally we would go and help herd the cattle. But the weekends would be pure entertainment, usually laden with weddings or soccer games. We would attend both competitive and casual games. All in all it was pure heaven, pure euphoria and pure adventure.

As you can see, our visit to our grandparents was a typical rural experience and pure joy. Especially for a young boy from the city..... it was heaven on earth!

As we grew, however, we began to like different things and he was not someone you could describe as spiritual. Well, if truth be told, he was bit of menace and liked his drink, just to give a 'brief' description of his quite interesting, if not notorious character. But I loved him all the same and our bond was strong and unbreakable. So when I heard he died after short illness I was heartbroken. My childhood comrade and co adventurer had gone. He was not just my cousin he was my brother!

His funeral and burial took place in the very same village we both enjoyed as young siblings. As African tradition would have it the tombstone would only be put after a year or so when 'the ground settles'.

Anyway here I was at the tombstone unveiling service, carefully listening to the preaching and following the proceedings.

Eulogies were given by his daughter and family and many other friends. Then they called his mum who was my aunt, Aunt Elsie, a younger sister to my mum. What she spoke blew me away.... listen with me.....

'I stand here today to give testimony about my son Thoko. Though a day of sorrow I stand comforted because of how he died. Thoko is our first born son. In his early days he was a good boy just like any other. However, as he grew he started to change. Especially when he went to secondary school, that's when he succumbed to peer pressure and he changed in personality and attitudes towards things such as drinking, smoking and he even assaulted his friends on occasion. He changed, not for the better but for worse. As a result, we were very concerned with his behavior as his parents . He lived this life for many years and we tried to give him all sorts of discipline as parents do, but to no avail. It dawned on us that we can't change him in our own power and realized that only God can change a man's heart. I started to pray and petition God, saying, 'God change my son! Change my son oh God, change my son'.

Now, when you want to 'stand in the gap' for someone you have to give yourself for them and almost lose yourself. I reached that state, and I would leave secretly in the night and climb Bunda Mountain which is on the outskirts of the city. Walking 2km deep in the night, I would hike the mountain alone to find a spot to pray and pour out my heart to God. I would pray that,

'Lord, he hasn't come home today and I have no idea where he is but you do! I pray that even if you allow his body to be harassed by sin or any sinful practices, I pray that you preserve his soul! Let the enemy beat his body but please preserve his soul.'

I prayed this prayer for years and years but there was no change until I had to change my prayer. My next prayer was that,

'Please do not allow my son to die without knowing you Jesus'.

I would often come home and see that his quarters have no lights and I would pray that 'Lord, wherever my son is, please preserve his life! Please preserve his soul! And do not take him from this word before he knows you Jesus. I wouldn't sleep whenever he was out. I would stay awake until around 3 or 4 am until I saw the lights in his house. Then I would know that my son is back home. I lived many years without sleep anxious about my son's safety and whereabouts. And whenever he returned I would kneel down and pray 'Lord thank you that my son is home, and has returned alive'.

When I left for work in the morning, I would meet my friends and wear a smile as if all was well, but deep within me a war raged on as I battled for my son's soul. This war raged on until in 2015. Now, on 23 June I was in a prayer service and the preacher gave a word of knowledge about me. He said

'God has given me a message for you. God says for the next 21 days you should not ask anything from God but you should only thank, worship and praise him'.

On, 13 July 2015, the last day of my fast I went to pray and returned home. I would always go to his house and talk to him and greet him, 'How are you my son?' But this was only possible if he had come home that night, and if he wasn't home I would simply get into his house and pray for him and then I would proceed to work.

On my way from work, I would again go to his quarters... if I found out that he had returned and was around. I would again say hello and find out about his day. We would chat on one or two things and I would proceed to the main house. But some days where not as civilized as they sound. Now 'Frustrated me', would at times lash out at him rebuking him for the bad habits of alcoholism and his related vices. But whenever Frustrated Me said these things to him he would always say

'Mum I love you, no matter how much you rebuke me or shout at me or say anything bad to me, I can't retaliate and answer you, you are my mum and I love you'.

This would always encourage me that despite his troubles his love for me is strong and his goodness is still in there somewhere.

This is something he would always say. But on this final day of my fasting for some reason I forgot to check on him when going to work. I only remembered to check on him in the evening.

'How are you my son?'

'Hi mum, I'm not doing too good today, I feel like I coming down with malaria'

I called his dad and asked him to buy some malaria medication at the pharmacy. On Tuesday the 14th I also went for prayers and responded to an altar call for those who were sick. I went to be prayed for and was asked what the problem was. I said 'it's not me it's my son, he has malaria.'

On Wednesday I went to the village with his Father and checked on him in the evening. He was doing quite well that day as he continued his medication. When we checked on him we asked how his day had been and how he was feeling. What he answered me astounded me and its undiluted meaning is in the vernacular Chichewa language he used. He responded

'A mami, kufa sipatali, ndikofunikila kuti ndikonze moyo wanga'

As Aunt Elsie explained her story, I tried to make sense of Thoko's words. Now the Chewa language is not as rich as other languages. It's mostly an equivocal one with different meanings to the same words depending on the context. But because of this unique feature, the language can be cryptic, inadvertently, or deliberately so.

Because of this fact there are several possible meanings to what Thoko said, the first is,

'Mum, death can happen anytime it's important for me to get my life back on track'

Or

'Mum, life is fragile and it's important for me to put my house in order'

These are the normal interpretations of what Thoko was saying especially since in this context he was doing well and on the road to recovery. Even such a realization was a great achievement for him. The reaction you would get when you hear of such a thing is to say 'that's deep, even for you Thoko, well done, that's deep'. After musing on this matter, my mind returned to Aunt Elsie as she continued her story.....

So knowing my son, I laughed at the fact that he had such an 'aha' moment and continued to nurse him. And he continued to say

'I need to change my life, I need to change, I don't go to church, I drink and smoke, I stopped going to church a long time ago and I really need to change, is the pastor available?' (I had found a pastor to be assisting him and counseling him from time to time)

'Yes he is'

'Can I please meet him so he can pray with me, please tell him I need to meet him'.

I ran to my phone and called the pastor saying

'Pastor, my son is calling for you, he wants to meet you'

'No need to delay here, however since it's already late I will be there first thing in the morning'

Even he knew that he should not miss this opportunity, all those tears, prayers and counseling was somehow paying off and if he was having a change of heart it was an opportunity not worth missing.

The next morning I went out to do a few things and did not bother calling the pastor. 'After all, he said he will call me when he comes', I thought.

On my return from my errands I decided to check on the pastor and see when he would pitch up.

'Pastor, you said you would come, where are you?'

'But I already came and was told you had gone for some errands. I had a good chat with your son. Everything about his life, he has told me. It is well with him don't worry about him!'

I wondered at his words, why was he saying I shouldn't worry about him, not knowing that God specifically told him to tell me those words 'don't worry about him'. And that God had shown him that Thoko will not recover.

I again went for prayers that day and there was a word of knowledge from the pastor there.

'Your son will die' he said! I was shocked and afraid. I started crying, yes, right there and then, literally stopping to pray and starting to cry. With all the people around me also stopping to pray and looking at what was wrong with me.

Then I figured, crying won't help me, I need to pray over this. And I prayed, passionately, fervently and with abundant faith. Rebuking the spirit of death, I prayed, asking for and commanding healing mercies from heaven'.

Then I started to praise God for healing mercies. I went home and decided in my heart that I will celebrate because I believed my son was no longer dying.

I went home and in true Malawian tradition decided to have a special meal that day. (Now when Malawians are happy or it's a special event, they won't have the normal corn flour based meal. They will usually have a rice meal with a popular soda drink by the side.)

'I decided to buy rice that day but did not have the money for it. I asked for K1,000 which was about $1.25 but no one had it. I went into the house and searched for rice and only found a handful of rice, literally a single scoop of rice that could fit into my one hand, in an old sack. And I say said to myself, everyone else will have nsima (normal staple food) but I will have this rice.

I started cooking while Thoko was chatting with his friend who had come to see him. I then took his portion of rice and gave it to him to eat and came back to my house. As I was about to dish out my food, I found his missed call on my phone and I ran to him.

'What's wrong my son,

'Mum my head is aching, I have a splitting headache'

I called the pastor who prayed for him over the phone, a powerful and anointed prayer, and afterwards I gave him some pain killers. And he said he was feeling better.

I felt at rest and did not take him to hospital

After supper, I went to sleep but debated within me, 'should I be his guardian tonight? But he had already had his brother as a guardian' so I slept.

I woke up at 3 am and wondered whether I should check on Thoko.

But I told myself that his brother would have told me if he was not well since he is the guardian tonight. So I went back to sleep. The moment I went back to sleep I heard a voice

'Wake up and go see your son'

So I woke up and went to his house. I didn't want to open the door and said let me listen from the window if he is fine or not because I might disturb him if he is sleeping. Then I heard him groaning and moaning, and I started crying 'my son, my son, oh dear God! My son.'

I rushed in the house

'What's wrong my son'

'Oh mum, my head, oh my head, mum let's go to hospital'

Ever since he was born my son was never admitted to a hospital and this was the very first time I ever had to take him to hospital.

Hurriedly, I called his dad and we took him to hospital. Praying all the way there. Once the night-shift doctors knocked off, my son was not attended to any more, all the doctors that came in the ward seemed to deliberately avoid him and skip his bed, if they came from the left, they would skip his bed and go to the next bed, if they came from the right they again skip his bed alone.

I just held on to prayer and said

'God I want his life'

The doctors never attended to him until, sadly, he died that morning.

Then several words started coming back to me. First the pastor said 'don't worry about him, it is well with him'.

Then Thoko's own words came to life and gave their true meaning

'A mami, kufa sipatali, ndikofunikila kuti ndikonze moyo wanga'

'Mum death is not far, I need to put my house in order' in other words

It dawned on me that he was actually bidding farewell and saying

'My death is not far, I am dying and will not recover, so I need to put my house in order'

I have been mourning my son's death quite a lot. I have been distraught and an emotional wreck, until in 2017 when I got another comforting message from God. There was a young lady who went to heaven in a vision and came back with a message. She told me that

'Mum, Jesus has sent me with a message that from today, don't ever worry about your son. Because your son is with Jesus. And I was asked to tell you that, 'when he was telling me this he was smiling."

I recalled one of the visions I myself had during the funeral I saw my son in the heavens, for a brief moment, and he was smiling. I was not too sure of what I was seeing so I kept it to myself.

The young lady continued to say, 'your son did not do well on this earth, but God had mercy on him because of your prayers. You have been praying that your son should not die without receiving Jesus as Lord and savior. So Jesus told me to tell you that as I speak you should know that he is in heaven.'

Therefore, as I share this testimony I want you all to know that this memorial service is for somebody who has been received into God's kingdom. Some of us think we can live our lives the way we want and still get to heaven. Well, let me tell you, there are no shortcuts to heaven especially if you don't fear God. For my son to be saved it required a lot of sacrifice. Firstly, the sacrifice of Jesus on the cross, secondly my own sacrifice of relentless prayer and fasting. I could fast up to 40 days until I could see all my veins showing through my skin.

Sometimes, when we pray we feel that God is not hearing and answering but he is. I have shared my testimony because I want to encourage you that if God gave me the grace to snatch my son from the jaws of hell, then God can do the same for you. And my desire is that I too will go to paradise and that all of you and all of us should see the glory of heaven!

So keep praying, keep striving in prayer and God can do marvelous things in your life and the lives of your loved ones.

5

Tamanda

A trip to heaven

On a bright Sunday morning 19 March 2017, in the midst of an anointed service, people were busy praising and worshiping God. The atmosphere was electric and drenched with the presence of God. Tamanda a young lady poured her heart wholly to God. She was gifted with the spirit of prophecy, revelation and word of knowledge and this gift would activate often as she would be used and moved by God to edify the church.

Then, she suddenly felt the urge to move to the front near the pulpit. She walked to the front as everyone was deeply engrossed in prayer and praise. Her hands were up and as she stood in the midst of others at the podium, she was slain by the spirit and fell down. This was 9 O'clock in the morning. She was taken into the ministry room where people prayed for her until 10 pm when she regained consciousness. What happened to her was strange because she did not really show any signs of responsiveness and as the narrator observed, she actually looked and seemed lifeless, but also looked like she had fainted but overall was completely unresponsive. When she regained consciousness she seemed a little restless and had to be calmed down until she was stable. The pastor would normally have first aid personnel to check on people and ensure they are fine or need medical attention, however on this day the pastor did not panic, he was actually told by God that I will visit you in a special way today and I will take one of your flock to heaven. He did not know who it was exactly but once Tamanda seemed to be "slain" in the spirit he immediately knew what was going on. Even the prayers were not necessary against any spiritual attack but were to pray for God's will to be done in that place.

On 21 March she was again at the prayer meeting and felt of sharing her story. So she started sharing her experience of all she had seen, from morning at about 9 am till 10pm. And so the story goes...

'When I fell I saw two angels come to me, one stood at my head and the other at my feet. I saw them take me and I left my body. I was told that I was unable to respond to people as they took me from the church after I was under the power of the God. I think it's because I had left my body, I was not in it, and I was not there! The angels took me to several places around the world. First I was taken to bars and pubs, I saw people getting drunk, dancing and having ungodly fun and happiness. Then I saw Jesus beside me and I saw him drop a tear from his eyes. I was also taken to hotels, motels and rest houses. Jesus said 'do you see these people, do you see what they are doing, if only they knew, their reward they would not be doing this.

The next place I was taken to was to a church, a very large church with a big following. Jesus told me 'look inside the church'. I looked inside but I saw a very heavy darkness. So I asked Jesus,

'How come people are devoutly praying and yet there is such a deep darkness?'

'It's because whatever is happening here is of their own making, it is not of me' answered Jesus.

I was taken to another church and shown a pastor. I will not reveal the identity of the pastor to you, because it is a big church. When we went into the church we saw the pastor praying and he was quite dramatic in his prayer. He would 'blow' on the people and the people would fall to the ground.

He seemed so anointed until Jesus said 'look at his hand'. And when I looked at his hand I saw beheld a sight I could never have imagined. I saw a big venomous serpent one that was so fearsome and long. Spanning from his hands at shoulder level all the way to his toes.

So when he would blow on people, he would move his hand and this snake would release power, biting them, poisoning and blinding their spirits, and they would fall to the ground in quite a dramatic way.

Jesus, again, said to me 'you see what's happening here is not of me, it looks like church but it's not of me'.

After that, we started ascending. We were not flying but were climbing a staircase into the heavens. Every step we took propelled us higher and higher and it seemed we were moving faster and faster until we came to a large road that had a smaller road branching off it. Within seconds we saw a multitude of people on the road. Jesus told me they were 3000 in total. In a moment the whole group, save 3, were taken on the large road as if swept by a large gush of wind. Only 3 people took the narrow road.

Jesus said

'Do you see this?'

'Yes Lord

'Come here let me show you the end of the large road

So we reached a place that was ever receiving people and ever expanding, and ever swallowing them. There, we heard ear piercing shrieks and cries. There was so much suffering there. I saw that they continued their sinful earthly works, whoever was in prostitution continued it, but they would do it in so much pain and suffering. Whoever died old was old but was disintegrating, and continued their earthly sins but in so much pain. They suffered so much but never died. They just suffered and suffered.

I looked at Jesus and to my surprise he did not shed a tear and his countenance was not as distraught as he was on earth. I was so heartbroken at their suffering, and thought of how touched Jesus was when we saw the various places on earth, and how he shed tears when he saw the people. I imagined how much more he would be touched and cry for those in hell.

I felt I needed to come to the bottom, of this and asked Jesus

'Lord when you showed me the different places on earth and the people deep in their sin, you cried for them and yet I don't see you crying for these people in hell. Why?

'I was weeping for those people on earth because they have an opportunity to make a choice and repent of their sin, but these ones have no longer any chance of changing and avoiding this suffering. So even if I cry it's for no purpose. For them their fate is sealed, they no longer have any chance of being saved.'

'Oh it's such a terrible place Lord.

'It is

'Can you show me at least one relative of mine who is here

'What good will that do? I won't show you a relative but I will show you my own servants.

Jesus brought up the spirit of one of his servants before me and said,

'Do you see this man, he was a powerful and anointed man of God. In fact he led so many people to me and many are in heaven because of him.

'But why is he here Lord? Such a powerful servant of God!

'He is here because his wife committed adultery and when she committed adultery she pleaded for his forgiveness but he was so angry at her that he never forgave her. He divorced her and remained angry at her until he died in his anger and unforgiving spirit..... Because of his unforgiveness, that's why he is in this place.

He brought another one and said,

'Do you see this man? He was a powerful servant of God but he is here because of unpaid debts. His debt was not even big to him but he took it for granted and did not care to even pay pack the person he had borrowed from. He also bought some things on credit and never paid back and took his debt, albeit small, for granted.

We continued on our journey and saw many other places and we went to another level of heaven and there were people who were looking young and strong and energetic, happy and joyful, and all were praising the Lord.

'Who are these Lord' I asked

'These are people who were doing my will on earth.

'At least now that we are in heaven can you show me my relative please?

'No, but I will show you one of my servants.... do you see this person she was a musician. The songs she wrote and sang were by divine inspiration, the songs were a means of serving people, sharing my word and filling them with hope and strength. There were a few others that God showed me and also he showed me how they faithfully served God.

God even took me to a place in heaven where I saw the patriarchs and prophets, I saw father Abraham and Moses. But all in all he told me that we should continue to serve God faithfully and God takes record of our good deeds.

But before I returned, Jesus gave me a message for Aunt Elsie here. Aunt Elsie, Jesus told me to tell you that he heard the prayer you had been praying for your son. You have been praying that God should not take him before knowing Jesus as Lord and personal savior, and as I speak now your son is in paradise with Jesus. Jesus deliberately took Thoko's life so that he should not return to his sinful ways. Your son would have recovered very well because he was not very ill and it was not his time, but God looked at the battles of life he had and knew that he would most likely forsake his new found faith in God.

—— As my aunt Elsie narrated this story to me she said, I had never told anyone in the fellowship about my prayer for my son, but when she said this I recalled a brief vision that I had at my son's funeral. As I sat by his casket, I saw my son high in the heavens and he was smiling at me, with a face so bright like that of the sun. Previously, I was so anxious of his salvation, knowing the type of person he was, but it's only in the village that I knew that my son is now in a good place.

As I heard her say this, I remembered how she explained her own version of Thokozani's story. How she prayed and fasted. She also mentioned the vision and the smile. What was going through Thoko's mind as he smiled can only be left to the imagination. But surely he looked at his mom and perhaps Jesus told him why and how he used his mom to pray for him.

How the love of Jesus was relentless through the relentless and unconditional love of a mother, how grateful he must have been to God and how grateful he must have felt to his mum, the smile was a mixture of myriad emotions that only a favored and forgiven sinner can feel. That only an unconditionally loved child can understand.

Yes others would judge him, in fact as I remember it, his funeral was not really supported that well by the church, he was not an ardent church goer after all, but as per church protocol and, effectively, in judgment, not many supported aunt Elsie on her son's funeral, the church and community responded in kind as they considered what manner of person they thought Thoko was.

I see this as a tendency of most churches. We are 'clicks' and 'clubs' anyway, but what saddened me the most was that in judgment of a person who had died, the church failed to cover and comfort fully, those who had been left behind, their own member faithful and dedicated, she together with her husband were the ones who needed the church's covering, comfort and strength, sometimes we overlook this and in our own self-righteousness we hurt and alienate our very own, we fail to see that there are always two sides to any death, the person who has died, whether good or bad, and the wounded that remain, the ones who bear any judgment and shame are not the ones who have left us, in fact they would care less, if at all, but we should serve and minister to those who are wounded, confused and bereaved amongst us.

So may God grant us wisdom in this regard, may we never forget that there is a special blessing for those who mourn and it is that 'blessed are those who mourn, for they shall, be comforted'.

If the church does not comfort them, God cannot be found a liar, he will comfort them himself. And that's exactly what happened to my aunt Elsie and that's exactly what happens to many others.... Jesus himself strengthens and comforts them.

As Aunt Elsie continued to explain this testimony, she said the message from Jesus continued —

'Your son would have recovered but God saw the ambush and traps of the devil that were laid in his path, your son was not very ill, but if he had recovered Satan was so thirsty for his soul, lying in wait, that the moment he would slip up and fall short in any way, Satan would assault him with sudden death, such as an accident or other calamity, all in order to destroy his soul.

At the time of his illness Thoko had realized the state of his sinful, pathetic life and soul and was repentant. Satan was not amused with this, because Thoko was firmly in his clutches for a long time and he was not happy to lose such a soul. Aunt Elsie, when Jesus was saying this, he was smiling, this is the message that I have been given to tell you regarding your son but he also gave me another message and said that as you have prayed for your son, you should also pray for others in your family. I have set you up in your family and clan so you can also pray for others and their children so they too may receive the grace and protection of heaven, because, such miracles of salvation only happen with much prayer and God's mighty Spirit'.

6

Enock

A Christmas gift from God himself

Rachel was married to a remarkable man in the name of Enock. She told her story and so it goes....

My story started in 1968 when I gave my life to Jesus. The person who led me to God, told me something so unique and special that I cherish and remember to this day. She said 'today you have been born again, God is your Father and you are now a child of God'.

That evening I went to God and prayed. I said 'God... now today I am your child, I want you therefore to give me your child for a husband. Someone who is saved and loves you so much that we can serve you together'.

This was on 28 August of that year. And as the year drew to a close, I met my husband on 25th December of the same year. He proposed to marry me on that very day. He told me how he grew up and how he got saved. He grew up in such an abusive home where his mother was forced into early marriage. He had a poor relationship with his abusive father who did not care for him and after all the pain he really did not have much. So he said,

'when you are saying yes to me you should know that I have

completely nothing, I have no education, no house, I have no job and no possessions'.

I told him that

'I am not marrying your possessions or wealth or education, I am marrying you as a person. You are my gift from the Lord, because on Christmas Day people give each other gifts and the Lord has given you to me on this special day'.

Fast forward to December 2020, God gave me a word in a vision, this word was shown written in the midst of a rainbow. Within the colors was written, "The joy of the Lord is your strength". I didn't know why this scripture was given to me but soon my husband became ill and was diagnosed with an infection which was later discovered as a kidney problem in its early stages. Soon after this diagnosis he was also diagnosed with Covid-19.

One day after my morning devotions I heard a word that said 'be strong and courageous, for you will take this people into the Promised Land'. I went to the bedroom where my husband was and I asked God that,

'Lord, are you saying you are going to take my husband?'

A few days later we took him to hospital on a Monday as his Covid-19 condition worsened. On our way to the hospital the Lord spoke to me and said,

'as he is being taken to hospital, know that he will not come back to the house again'. When I heard this I remembered the word in the rainbow and the scriptures from the book of Joshua that I had received before, and I simply said,

'Lord let your will be done'.

That Monday, Enock was in a general ward and on Tuesday he was taken to the isolation ward. That meant we could not visit him as he was now in intensive care requiring constant monitoring and oxygen therapy. On Thursday evening the doctor asked my granddaughter and said 'would you like to talk to your grandfather?' We said 'yes' and the doctor used video calling so we could speak to him. Sadly, he could not speak but at least we saw him. The Lord confirmed to me that 'he is to speak to you no more but you have a chance to at least see him before his time comes'.

On Friday morning as I was outside the house, the Lord spoke to me saying 'Do you remember on 28 August 1968 you asked me to give you a husband? And on the 25th of December I gave you a husband, now it's your turn. I am asking you to give me back your husband.'

I was stunned and speechless! I knew God had warned me about Enock's demise but I guess it hadn't really sunk in. I think that deep down below I was still processing the message and perhaps remotely wished it wasn't true or at least not so soon, not today at least! So, speechless, and completely dumbfounded, I did not respond God. However after recollecting myself I responded to Him and said 'your will be done'.

Later that day, one of my daughters living in the United Kingdom called me to tell me the prayer that her daughter had prayed that morning. She said my daughter prayed 'God send your angels to go and get grandpa'.

I realized this was no coincidence, she would not call if she thought this was mere childhood babble. I said to her, 'she is a great intercessor and is praying according to what God has shown her. We will take her word and wait upon the Lord'.

The next morning at 7 o'clock in the morning we got news from the hospital that my husband had just passed on.

By this time I was somewhat prepared because of all that God had told and shown me. I had also prepared my daughters and granddaughters by sharing my experiences with them.

But God spoke to me again that 'be prepared that people are going to shun you because of Covid-19' this was also because I was also diagnosed with it. But on the day he died God gave me such peace in my heart. Even when people were coming to mourn with me, I was still full of peace and joy in my heart because God asked me to give him back to him'.

Indeed I was shunned, and the Covid-19 burials were very swift which did not allow for enough time to mourn and process everything that had happened. People were afraid to talk to me or come near me and even fewer people managed to visit us freely in the home. But God had already warned me of this and I accepted the situation as a result of the times we live in.

I recall that I previously used to visit widows and one favorite verse I used to share with them was Isaiah 54:5 that 'God your creator is your husband'. On this day I was reminded of this scripture and God spoke to me again saying 'you are not a widow because I, your maker am your husband! And your children are not orphans, I their maker am their father'.

I was therefore confident enough to pray and I told God that

'Lord you know how my husband treated me and how he loved me and how he provided for everything, and he only knew me in part and yet you know me deeper and are a more perfect husband, much more than him, so you have to take full responsibility for my life'.

Four days after the burial, God reminded me of the ministry for widows and he said 'you were doing this ministry with your husband but now the baton has been passed to you'.

Now I know that God wants me to strengthen other people who are also experiencing the same pain and loss that I am feeling. I thank God that He strengthened me and even prepared me for the transition of my husband and that he was with me all the way and still walks with me and strengthens me to this day.

My hope is and remains in God.

7

Dorcas

Strengthened and sustained by a sovereign God

Dorcas was a last born in a family of 11 and had a rich spiritual background. In fact, her father was Uriah Chirwa. Now this is no ordinary name in the annals of Malawian history. He was one of the righthand men of Robert Laws. Robert laws, if I must remind you, was a Scottish missionary who spread the gospel of Jesus in the northern region of Malawi in a place called Livingstonia. He headed the Livingstonia mission for 50 years and it played a crucial role in educating Africans during the colonial era.

It is said that he committed to being a missionary after listening to a powerful sermon by Robert Moffat in the year 1865 and hearing and inspired by the stories of Dr. David Livingstone's travels to Africa. The Livingstonia mission he established is there to this day together with a University.

Uriah Chirwa worked with Robert Laws and was therefore instrumental in the work of the missionary. Uriah was trained, through the mission, to be an ordained minister but for some reason was never ordained. The family says that he refused to be ordained and until this day it is not known why he refused. What is known, however, is that he remained key and instrumental in serving and setting up the mission at Robert Laws.

So, Dorcas had this progeny of faith oozing through her veins. She was not an outspoken person, not at all and in those days there was no Charismatic movement whereby one would claim being born again and filled by the spirit, she was simply known as someone who had a simple faith in the basic Gospel which said 'Jesus died for our sins and if we accept his sacrifice, our sins will be forgiven and we will receive the gift of eternal life'. It was nothing complicated but you could see this faith growing up in her and changing her. As her grandson, Frank, told me her story, he recalls that at one time she got so despondent with the challenges and pain she had experienced in her life. A string of tragedies of death and sickness, resulting in the death of her siblings had started to weigh on her spirit and she started to lose hope.

As a last born, you look up dearly to your siblings, they are your hope and inspiration. They challenge you to do better and be like them, but one of the most painful things is to see these same dearly beloved brothers and sisters die before your eyes. They were born 11 in their family only 2 boys and 9 girls, and she was the last of them all. As a last born there are several things you are characterized by. First is favor, because you're the youngest of them all and the jewel of your parents. So you do get it a bit easy sometimes but also there is a trait that is so hidden that it may not be recognized at all. You grow in the spirit of servitude as you support and help your siblings, we see it in the life of Joseph when he would serve his brother's with supplies as they took care of their father's flock, we also see the same spirit in David as he was the only one left to tend to his father's sheep while his brothers were at war and also when he was asked to bring them food and supplies in the midst of battle in Saul's army.

A spirit of service can lead to unlocking great things as we saw in the life of David. In serving he encountered a great opportunity to fight Goliath. In the story of Joseph, his service led to other things, he actually suffered for his integrity of telling on his brothers when they were plundering their fathers flock. While we normally see Joseph as perhaps a spoiled last born who was indeed unfairly favored, he is someone who paid the price for his integrity, and both his integrity and servitude put his life on a trajectory he never imagined, and yet it was all God working in his situation.

So here was Dorcas, another last born. As her grandson Frank tells her story, he came to know her better over time, he says he knew her first as bit of a difficult person and not very approachable. He was quick to say that he would avoid interacting with her but over time she had a gradual and certain change in character and temperament. When Frank was growing up as a young man he knew the difficult grandma Dorcas, but for some reason God gave them a special connection and he came to witness the living faith that literally changed her into a close friend of his. Her own husband was called Frank and she soon took special interest in him because he was a namesake of her husband. She would therefore call him 'Amuna anga' which literally means 'my husband'. In fact towards the end they became the best of friends to the extent that on Frank's wedding, on 5 April 2009, she was completely wild with joy and arguably more elated than everyone else. And, if truth be told, she loved Frank's wife, Chiku. Frank recalls the kind and heartfelt counsel where she said,

'please love one another, with your whole hearts, please be faithful to one another, Frank please cherish Chiku and Chiku please cherish Frank, you are a lovely couple and a pure blessing to each other'.

As Frank recalls, 'my grandma just became such a blessing, such an encouragement and a dear friend' until she died in 2017, she was such a blessing and encouragement'.

One of the things that Frank reminisced was that her life turned out really good but she hit a speed bump at some point in her life. At the time she was assaulted by a string of pain and death in her family one of these deaths was at a time when she, herself, was very sick to the point of death. She had lost all hope, was completely down cast and she even asked God to take her life.

She simply explained that God strengthened her at that time until she recovered from hospital and experienced many of God's blessing. At this time she was expecting a child who was Frank's uncle an elder brother to his dad. Had God not healed her, two children would not have been born, the last two boys of the family. She had had a string of girls and at the point when she wanted to give up and throw in the towel God had two boys waiting to be born. And if you look at this great blessing of two children, she would have missed out on the joy of not just these two boys but also of their grandchildren and Frank was one of them. In fact, she had so many grandchildren and God had this marvelous blessing for her when she felt she had come to the end of her road. Frank himself has the same blessing of a deep faith in Jesus, and shares in his great grandfather Uriah's spirit of serving a great man of God with a prophetic vision and gift for the nation of Malawi. While he may or may not be a right hand man since there are several who serve with him, he is surely a faithful and committed person in his service to God through the ministry of this esteemed minister. His cousins too, from his uncle are people of faith and share this blessed heritage. And Frank recalls that Grandma Dorcas reflected on all this and told him a secret to all this that only dear friends can know and share. She told him, 'my life has been such a blessing, but there is a secret to all this. Once I was so downcast because I was going through a lot of pain. I had lost several of my siblings in quick succession, and I also became very sick. I told God that 'all my siblings are dying, why is there so much pain and loss in this life? First was my siblings who are dying, and now I am battling this debilitating illness it's better if you take me too. I see no purpose in this life, I truly have nothing to live for'.

When I prayed this prayer it's because I had been sick for a very long time and I lost all hope of life, once I prayed this prayer, I had a dream in which I saw God and he said to me 'Ine ndine Mulungu, simdiweluzika, sungandiuze kuti ndikutenge, ndine Mulungu sindiweluzika'

(Meaning

'Ine ndine Mulungu, "I am God"

Sindiweluzika, "I am sovereign I cannot be judged or brought to answer to man"

Sungandiuze kuti ndikutenge, "you can't tell me to take your life"
ndine Mulungu sindiweluzika, "because I am God and I cannot be judged!")

God then told me that
"that in fact you won't die now and you will actually be the last one to die, you will see all your siblings die but you will be the last one to die."

Frank, look at me now, its 2006 and I am really the only one who is alive, I thought my life was over but look at what God can do! The sickness took a toll on me even when I was expecting a child and now I have many grandchildren that I would never have seen had I died at the time. Also, your dad and your uncle would not have been born and I would have missed out on knowing you my dear friend. I would also have missed out on knowing your darling wife and the joy of seeing you passionately serving God like this.

God's word is true, had he not strengthened me, I would not have been here today, I would have died had I not believed. I was told of the promise and purpose of God, now I know that only God is the king and owner of life, he is the sustainer and protector of our life. I pray that God will help me see you two get married one day. He has promised me long life after all. So I think I can still believe him for that amuna anga'.

As Frank confirms that Grandma Dorcas did indeed see him get married and even saw her great grandchildren. Dorcas died in 2014 after witnessing their wedding 3 years after this discussion and enjoying seeing the growth of their marriage 5 years into it.

And 13 years into their marriage by the time of this book, it is apparent that he misses her fondly and is grateful to God for his faithfulness to her.

So, are you at a low point in life? Do you think all is lost, are you also complaining to God that there is no point to life? Remember, he is

God, he can't be judged, and in fact he has something in store for you! Something special and beyond your wildest dreams.

8

Young Lives

The remarkable departure of Sayo, Nangwa and Sarah

Sayo was the chairperson of Young Lives (YL). They had a Young Lives trip in 2013 to Harare in Zimbabwe. Before the day of departure he asked his wife Joy to a dinner date even though it was already after work and he hadn't given notice.

Joy was so tired and truly did not want to go. All she wanted was to stay in and keep company in the house. After all, with most ladies they need forewarning early in the day and not abruptly, 1 hour before the date. How would she freshen up and look her best?

But Sayo would have none of it. He told her to put on her best clothes and make-up for this special evening, she did not want to, but he practically forced her to go. Being the loving and caring wife she was, she agreed and prepared for their special, albeit abrupt, evening.

Sayo took her to an expensive hotel and as they chatted away he jokingly brushed over the fact that he had settled all household bills and there was nothing she should be worried about. He proceeded to joke and say "so tomorrow I am going for this Young Lives trip and in case I don't come back I want you be happy and to marry again". Joy was shocked at this sentiment and asked "why are you talking of such things? You don't have to worry so just stop talking about it".

Normally in Malawi talking of death is a taboo amongst most Malawians. So, she too would have none of it! But Sayo insisted and jokingly said "but just in case I don't come back please do marry again! Just make sure he is not a hip-hop head like me. Coz that would be an insult to me since I am the ultimate hip-hop head there is! No one loves hip-hop more than me". So, Joy laughed it off and giggled the evening away with their snug romantic talk.

Meanwhile, their friend Nangwa was equally excited about the trip and he too thought he had some unfinished business. He had put off painting a wall in his house for so long and this evening he took up his tools, paint pan and roller in hand, and a paint bucket in the other, and started painting. His wife, Favor, asked him what are you doing why are you painting at such a time as this? To which Nangwa responded "No, I must do this I have put it off for so long and I now need to finish it".

Favor tried to put him off but he insisted 'I must do it today at all costs!' And the next morning, before leaving, the Young Lives group spent a few minutes in their usual time of prayer to consecrate the journey.

Then they started off, on their expedition to Zimbabwe, on a 750km drive to Harare. It was a lovely trip and the scenery was beautiful. But they were late. The driver had to catch up with the border closing times and hand to ensure that they got out of Malawi and into Mozambique. And then out of Mozambique in just enough time before the 6pm border closing time. So, he stepped on the gas! As he sped along in the 18-seater bus the passengers started complaining of their safety and asked the driver to slow down and be more careful. At this, Sayo, in his joking tone said 'ife tatsanzika kale m'makwathumu ndiye tilibe bvuto' (some of us have already said our goodbyes in our homes so we have no problem!'). So keep it up driver! And Nangwa also stepped in and said 'enafe zathu zonse zilibwino tikafa pano tikudziwa kumene tikupita' (for some of us all our affairs are in order and if we die now, we know where we are going!).

They were not alone as a local bunch because in their company they also had Sarah, a Young Lives missionary from the USA who was on a visit to Malawi. She was just listening to these crazy dudes and giggled along with them. As any modest lady would do.

Continuously joking they, they sped along and made their journey to the Zimbabwe boarder, just making it for the 6pm border crossing and later making it in the dead of night in the city of Harare. Tired and exhausted they settled in and enjoyed the rest of the program.

The conference was anointed and so uplifting. But as surely as the sun rises, the day to go back home certainly came. They could not believe it, they wanted to go on with the conference, but time had flown by so fast. All the "hallelujahs" were done and the "amens" were said. It was time to take the long journey back home. Excited and energized blessed and drenched in the uplifting word of God they set off on their arduous journey.

Before setting off, they had their usual time of Bible reading and then meditation on what had been read. They would normally all share what they felt God was speaking to them in their time of personal study and reflection, and so they did.

One by one they climbed back into the bus. The diesel engine roared to life, as the bus pulled out of the campus and went on its way, there was a calmness as everyone reclined in their seats, watching the beautiful countryside of the nation of Zimbabwe. As they moved along traveling at speeds that will help both arrive safely but also beat the borders. They watched the rocky countryside that is so characteristic of this beautiful land. After all, it is called "Zimbabwe the land of rocks".

Peacefully they sped along... the driver seemingly had a better grip on how to gauge his speed and distance, after all they were early so there was not much to rush for this time around, but as with all long road trips, they needed to maintain a descent speed.

Then, as fate would have it, tragedy struck! Bang! Bang!! Loud ear-deafening sounds were heard! From nowhere the Young Lives team saw the world revolving and spinning around them. They wondered what was happening as they saw the bus leave the road, and the frame of the bus spinning before their very eyes!

The luggage bags they had were airborne and, as if in a movie, they could see themselves suspended in midair. Then bang! Thud! And crunch! They were thrown from side to side as they collided with the frame of the bus. Then, an eerie silence! The bus had finally come to a halt...

Dazed and confused, the team could hear cries and shouts of their friends who had been disillusioned by the traumatic ordeal. Looking around they saw the bus wrecked and badly damaged. They saw the two front tires totally burst and destroyed, and it, only now, made sense of the first deafening bangs they had heard. This had made the driver lose control and veer off the road. Failing to control the vehicle they rolled and the bus overturned 3 times.

But wait a minute where was everyone? As sanity somewhat returned, it dawned on the team to check on themselves and see if they were all ok. Looking around they saw 3 of their friends lying on the ground motionless!! "Oh no" they thought "who is this" coming closer, bracing with the gory scene of bruises and blood, there they were!

It was Sayo, Nangwa and Sarah their missionary, the lady who silently giggled about her readiness to go to heaven! Alas! They had lost three beautiful souls; full of life and full of energy. It was so confusing as to why this could happen to such god fearing and completely sold-out passionate souls!

And that was the demise of three young and beautiful souls. The confusion on their loved ones was immense but somehow, very inexplicably, they made it through this tough season and buried their loved ones. However, their memories live on in their hearts.

As I gathered and listened to this story, I felt that "if this be the end of the story, it leaves me all confused and bewildered, there must be more I thought?"

But how would I ever know? I would need to resign to the sad fate of pain and worry, clinging on to the faith we all have that perhaps they were ready to go or indeed that as long as we believe in God we have a promise of heaven.

But some months later, one youth Pastor, David Kalilani, was on a trip to Tanzania to preach the word of God at a church called 'Oceans' and yes you guessed it, it was on the shores of the Indian ocean.

During his preaching he talked of this Young Lives team and how God had taken them to heaven and drawing lessons of how important it is to serve God while we still have life as these young people did. After he preached there stood a white man called Steve from the USA explained that he was actually the "boss" of the said Young Lives team operating from their HQ in USA and that he actually knew all three of them. He went on to say that the night before the Young Lives team had an accident he had a dream.

In his dream he saw Nangwa, Sayo and Sarah in an extremely beautiful and glorious place, shining and bright, extremely peaceful and serene. Then they all said to him "come here and be with us. It so lovely here!" To this he said "no I can't come just yet, I have things to do so I will join you guys later".

Waking up the next morning Steve was so confused as to what the dream could mean. The next day he shockingly heard of the accident. He added that on the day of departure the Young Lives team had their usual meditation as explained by the Pastor and it is in this time of meditation that Nangwa was shown a vision. In this vision he saw a big hand coming down from heaven reaching out to his hand. Then a voice was heard asking 'are you willing?' to which Nangwa answered 'yes I am willing!' Nangwa then saw this mighty hand pulling him from and into heaven and he saw himself steadily floating and then speeding at the speed of light, and faster, from the earth. He then looked behind him and saw two most interesting things. First, he saw two more people who had held on to his other hand following below him. He looked at them but could not make out their faces and did not know who they were.

The second peculiar thing was that below him was the country and nation of Malawi. What he saw was that it was a dry and arid land with no vegetation at all. His heart sank when he thought about his nation.

But then... very suddenly he saw little shoots of grass and vegetation start springing up from the dry and thirsty ground! And suddenly his vision was over. Startled at what he had seen, he shared the story to his friends who were equally perplexed and surprised at what could be its meaning.

Only after the death of these three souls did his vision and the vision of Nangwa make sense to him, and not only him but also to his friends. He explained that God had been preparing his Young Lives team and the families of the departed friends for them to know that they had not just died in vain but that they were actually in a better place. He further explained that God is doing something mighty in Malawi because the grass shoots and springing vegetation actually symbolize the revival that would come to Malawi in the hearts of his people.

Such was the remarkable departure of these young lives!

Brandon

A dark departure on a bright and sunny day!

Brandon was a troubled soul. He lived in the rural villages of Mzimba Malawi. Troubled in the sense that "he" was troublesome and his character brought him little friends, and he indeed was mostly troubled by his own vices.

He never got along well with other people and was the troublemaker of the community. He was one of the people who engaged in significant substance abuse. He was addicted to smoking marijuana and would need to steal and even thug people, just to fund his habit.

Now, this specific day was quite a bright sunny afternoon, with not a cloud in the sky, the perfect day, for all intents and purposes.

Then, all of a sudden, he started to complain of darkness. He was overcome by a gripping fear which was so unusual to the people around him as this was 'one mean dude' who would rarely scare!

He shouted to the people around him that 'Chonde yatsani nyali zanu ndikuona mdima' ('please switch on your lamps because I see darkness'). Confused and bewildered the onlookers thought it was one of his drunken episodes and simply watched in astonishment. If it were night time they would light their lamps but on the brightest day as this, there would be no such need!

But Brandon did not stop, he continued complaining and moaning. And his moaning quickly became grumblings and his grumbling became shouting and his shouting became shrieks that pierced the ears and hearts of the hearers and crowd that was, ever so quickly, gathering around him. Brandon remained restless and continued to ask for people to light their lamps.

He continued to see darkness and what he described as a strong sense of blackness around him and blackness that was quickly wrapping itself around him.

As he continued to battle with the darkness he saw it engulf him and overpower him. As he struggled, in broad day light! The crowd continued to gather around him in shock and amazement. Mostly in frustration, for failure to do anything that could help their colleague! Then as Brandon struggled he shouted loudly 'Nyali yanga ya thima! Nyali yanga ya thima' ('my candle has gone out! my lamp has gone out!')... And immediately he said this, Brandon fell down... dead!

Now the Bible says the "spirit of a man is the candle of the Lord". It also says hell is a place of everlasting darkness without the presence of the Lord. It would seem that the departure of Brandon showed signs of where he was going. Unfortunately it was not a good place but while for him his life was cut short, you and I still have an opportunity to receive salvation and atonement for our sins and also from all condemnation of hell. And as long as you have life you and I have hope!

So if you want to enter heaven you can say a salvation prayer in the chapter called : "A door to heaven" and you will received Jesus as your personal Lord and Savior, and the gift of salvation.

10

Mr. Gershom

The departure of a loving father and husband!

Mr. Gershom (actual name "Geresomu") lived in the village, somewhere in Mchinji district. He was actually my uncle and was quite a jolly fellow, one who had a living and personal faith in God. All he knew was the simple gospel, nothing fancy, nothing flowery, he was not even a Pentecostal guy, he was in a mainline traditional church but he held on to the truth that Jesus died for his sins in order that he may be forgiven and have eternal life.

It was enough for him to know that he made a personal decision to commit his life to Jesus and receive him as Lord and Savior. His gospel was not materialistic or motivational his gospel was purely spiritual.

Gershom complained of chest pains for a few days and he kept pushing it aside thinking it's one of those things that come and go on their own. But days turned into weeks and weeks into a few fortnights. After seeing that the cramps were persistent he was finally persuaded by his relatives and his wife to go to hospital. But certainly he could not have done so by himself. They are just overconcerned wimps, he thought to himself, and such was his character.

Reluctantly, he made the trip and got himself to the hospital. After explaining his symptoms to the doctor, they took him for some tests. He patiently waited for the tests and just by looking at the expressions on the doctors' faces he somehow knew that something was gravely wrong with him.

The results finally came back ...it was now the moment of truth. The doctor started explaining and they were not good. He was told he had a tumor in his chest and as if that was not enough it was cancerous. Taking the bitter news, he went back home. He reluctantly told his wife and family about his condition. It was tough for everyone, but they put their faith in God.

As his illness progressed he grew weaker and weaker from the pain, and finally he was admitted to hospital. He was soon in critical condition and completely bedridden with little mobility. He could not even sit upright or stand due to the pain.

Soon his pastor decided to visit him in hospital, As all caring pastors would. When Gershom saw his very reverend pastor he amazingly got up from his bedridden state and, to the bewilderment of all guardians sat up, got off the bed and hugged the Pastor. He seemed to be in unusually high spirits for a terminally ill patient.

Soon, the Pastor started to share words of encouragement and promises of Gods healing. In the midst of the preaching Gershom stopped the pastor and said "But pastor even though you are encouraging me, my journey is already set. Don't worry about me, I am going home! My house is complete in heaven and it is ready for me and my door is already open for me to go!"

He then started telling the pastor what to preach on his funeral. He gave two verses to the Pastor, namely Revelation 14:13 and Hebrews 4: 14-16.

Revelation 14:13 says:

'Then I heard a voice from heaven say, "Write this: Blessed are the dead who die in the Lord from now on. "Yes," says the Spirit, "they will rest from their labor, for their deeds will follow them."

Gershom wanted his family to know that he is blessed because he is dying in the Lord. And because he is dying in the Lord he is going to be with his master in heaven. He is going to a good place where his Lord has prepared a place for him. He also wanted his family to know that though he had labored on this earth he is going to a place of true rest in God.

He also had the hope of receiving a reward from the good labor and good works he did on this earth. He knew that his works will follow him and will be rewarded by God.

To his family he specifically wanted them to be encouraged by Hebrews 4:14-16. The passage talks of Jesus the Great High Priest who is standing in the gap for us. It says

'Therefore, since we have a great high priest who has ascended into heaven, Jesus the Son of God, let us hold firmly to the faith we profess. For we do not have a high priest who is unable to empathize with our weaknesses, but we have one who has been tempted in every way, just as we are —yet he did not sin. Let us then approach God's throne of grace with confidence, so that we may receive mercy and find grace to help us in our time of need.'

Gershom wanted his wife and children to know that they're not alone. Rather they have a high priest in Jesus who will stand in the gap when he is gone! He wanted his family not to doubt God but to hold firmly to the faith they confess and profess.

It is the most disheartening thing when children are orphaned. But, with Jesus standing in the gap, God truly becomes a father to the fatherless and defender of the widow.

Secondly, he wanted his wife and kids to know that Jesus is just like us. He is not some distant God who is not in tune with our feelings. He himself was tempted like we are. The Bible tells us that Jesus lost his father, Joseph at an early age. So, he wanted his family to know that Jesus understands their pain. He knows what it is to be tempted but he also knows what it is to be orphaned, to feel despair and loss and to feel empty and helpless. It is with this love and compassion that Jesus prays to God the Father on our behalf.

He also wanted his family to know that because of who Jesus is, and because of his love and compassion, they should not doubt when they approach God, they should not feel condemned when they are weak and tempted with hopelessness and despair. No, not at all, but that in times of weakness and little strength, they should still approach God! They should not only have faith but they should be brave, audacious and daring, in their requests to God. They should know they have a God who is big, a God who is rich, a God who owns the cattle on a thousand hills and above all, a God full of grace and mercy.

They should also remember that Jesus himself was an orphan. For the most part, he had no father because, as history tells us, his father, Joseph, died when he, Jesus was just a teenager! And at the cross of his crucifixion he only had Mary and even Mary had to be given a new home. Because as he hung on the cross , he looked to John and he told him 'son here is your mother' and 'mother here is your son', and the Bible tells us that John took his mother Mary into his home from that day onward.

So, Jesus himself knew the pain of being an orphan as a teenager. He knew the weight of responsibility on his shoulders, the need to provide for his family, not only because he had no father, but also because he had younger brothers to take care of and literally be a father to! He knew the discipline of providing for his family and siblings. He experienced the grace of God on the work of his hands to the extent that he, as a carpenter's son, used his skills to make money and support his family.

Now ... If Jesus, who was an orphan saw the grace of provision, Gershom's children could be equally confident that they will see the same grace and same provision, they would experience the same sustenance and protection that Jesus himself experienced.

Also, since Jesus both experienced orphan-hood and is also a high priest interceding on our behalf, he is the best person to intercede for us. His intercession comes from the same pain he experienced and therefore he knows how to ask grace from the Father!

Another important thing is that since Jesus still fulfilled his purpose in life despite his being an orphan. Then God can definitely fulfill his purpose in the lives of his children. What is there to stop them therefore from praying boldly to God? Nothing! Nothing at all!

Therefore, at all times they should not succumb to self-pity but they should hold their heads high and come before their heavenly Father, their defender and their sustainer.

They should be bold and almost arrogant about their requests. They should be audacious in their God! In addition to these two scriptures he also left two hymns one is titled "In Christ alone my hope is found" and the other "I have a home beyond the blue."

The lyrics of the first song say

"My hope is built on nothing less, Than Jesus Christ, my righteousness;
I dare not trust the sweetest frame, But wholly lean on Jesus' name.
On Christ, the solid Rock, I stand; All other ground is sinking sand,
All other ground is sinking sand"

Gershom was a loving father, a husband who by divine revelation reached out to his family and comforted them and prepared them for his departure. He really is a blessing for dying in the Lord and was particularly blessed with a bit of time to comfort his family. A bigger blessing it was for him to pick out such comforting and encouraging words not only to his family but to us all.

How Gershom Passed

Now how did my uncle Gershom actually die? Now that's the exciting part! On the day he was brought from home from his last hospital visit, he started asking to meet different people as if to see them for the last time. He had to put his affairs in order and managed to meet most of the people he requested for.

This included giving details of how he was to fulfill his church pledges and he particularly wanted to see his friend Edward for the last time. So, he asked "Please call Mr. Nkhwazi ("Edward") for me!"

Unfortunately he delayed and as he waited he continually said, "why is Edward delaying doesn't he know I am going home today?" At this his wife Jennifer knew that Gershom was passing on that day. But, how would Gershom say he is going home when he has already come home from the hospital?

Once Edward came Gershom asked, him, "Edward why are you delaying when I am calling you? Don't you know I am going home today? I want to bid farewell because I am going home today."

Jennifer immediately started crying, Gershom then reprimanded both her and Edward who were equally looking sullen. "Why are you sad? Don't you know I have a home?"

Don't be sad, I am going to a much better place, a more beautiful place so don't be sad because I have a home! I am going home this very evening and I will leave at 7 O'clock!" he said, with so much expectation and excitement.

But Jennifer was too distraught! And she continued to cry even more knowing that her husband will soon be gone. Gershom then asked everyone to remove his wife from the lounge.

"Please take her out of the house, why is she crying? Please take her outside the house, she will delay me".

Jennifer was crying because it was literally 5 minutes to 7 O'clock and what her husband was saying was not very encouraging in her view. Especially considering that it was almost 7 O'clock. Edward and other relatives then removed Jennifer as requested and as they calmed her down they went back to the lounge. At this point uncle Gershom laid back his head on the chair, closed his eyes and rested. Taking a deep breath as if falling asleep.

Everyone who remained watched and soon realized that Gershom was actually no more. He had stopped breathing, closed his eyes and his heart had stopped beating and when checked had no pulse... and.....it was just a few minutes after 7:00 pm!

11

Sarah

The departure of a faithful servant of God!

Sarah was an assistant pastor in Bible faith ministries. She was Assistant Pastor to my Pastor-friend McDonald who was heading their branch in Blantyre City. She was a powerful woman of faith who was very dedicated to God and to the Lord's service and though she was not yet ordained a pastor she was already given pastoral roles in the church. In fact, she was only in her final year of bible school where she was pursuing a Diploma in Theology.

In her three years of theological training she had a protracted and fierce battle with cancer. She was on and off, and in and out of hospital on multiple occasions. During this long battle she had a surgery in which the doctors had to remove the cancerous cells. After these surgeries the doctors decided to take her back to yet another surgery and they discovered that not all cancerous cells were removed in the initial surgeries.

Doctors then decided to put her on chemotherapy which was another painful part of the cancer journey.

Now, on Christmas Eve of 2009 Pastor McDonald was ready to

57

administer Holy Communion as was the church's custom for the season. But, remembering the situation of the assistant pastor, he and the church leadership decided to visit Sarah in hospital after the service.

On their way to the hospital McDonald received a call from Sarah saying that

'Pastor we have been discharged from hospital but I know that I am going home'.

McDonald was startled at this statement, *'I know that I am going home!'* and wondered what it meant.

It looked like she was not talking about her house or her village but was referring to something else and looked like she was talking about her heavenly home. Curious, McDonald could only keep this to himself and ponder it further. He decided to simply be there for her and cheer her up as much as possible.

From the hospital Sarah went straight to her home village in Chiradzulu district. As a result, McDonald could only visit her after Christmas since Sarah was no longer in town.

Little did McDonald know that this Christmas would be like no other, and indeed on the evening of the 25th of December he had a divine encounter! He had a vision that night, in which he saw an army of angels, 'A heavenly host' to use his exact words. And he saw many angels that had descended from heaven.

He saw worship instruments and types of angels he had never seen before and an indescribable beauty that he had never seen before! In the midst of this engulfing beauty and in the middle of the vast army, he heard the voice of God saying

'I am taking my servant home!'

McDonald did not know which servant was being taken home. He knew his assistant pastor was ill but could it be her?

"Perish the thought" he mused and said to himself, and he coupled this situation with passionate prayer, rebuking negative thoughts and all evil plans of the devil. After all, with God all things are possible.

Early in the morning of Boxing Day he called his senior pastor to tell him what happened to him. The Senior Pastor, said he had a strong sense that the servant in the vision is McDonald's very own assistant pastor. In disbelief, McDonald then called Sarah that very morning, but they could not converse for long as Sarah was very weak. He simply decided to visit her in the village. On arrival he asked her how she was keeping and she said,

'Pastor the pain is excruciating and terrible, but the peace I have is unspeakable. I have amazing joy and I have amazing peace all over, joy that I have never experienced before! I have battled sickness all these 3 years and been troubled with thoughts of why God would allow this to happen to me especially when I am a servant of God especially when I am praying and trusting in him to heal me. But all I have now is great peace and Joy! Even though I am in great pain my mind and my heart are at rest.'

Sarah's guardian's told McDonald that Sarah was not eating or talking. They wondered at how she had just started talking when he came and asked him to persuade her to eat something. And persuade her he did. She was reluctant and a bit difficult because she said food is delaying her and that it make's her feel heavy and that her body is just weighing her down. But McDonald insisted that at least she take a few scoops of porridge, "just for energy" and fortunately she accepted. She sat upright and was given some porridge that day.

They chatted for about an hour and a half and as he was about to leave, Sarah said

'my door has opened. Heaven is waiting for me!'

Stunned and startled McDonald did not know how to react, he had mixed feelings of sadness and joy at the same time. He also had a tinge of envy as he knew that Sarah was going home and to a good home for sure!

He recalled her faithful and diligent service. How she held on to God in times of trouble and her unwavering faith in God throughout her illness. McDonald wished he could follow her home. But his time had not come and all he could say was 'it is well'.

Once he got home he now started reflecting on the events of the day and he suddenly had thoughts of heaven engulfing his mind. This meditation was an appetizer of what would come and it gave him glimpses of heaven. So, he proceeded to pray for Sarah. But how would he pray? Humanly he was tempted to pray for her healing but knowing that God had already revealed that she would go home, he could only pray for the strengthening of the family.

Early on the morning of the 27th as if the first vision was not enough, McDonald had a repeat and continuation of the heavenly vision at around 3:30 am which was exactly the time of the first vision from the previous morning.

Now in this dream he saw what was like a decorated heaven. The colors were blue, gold and violet. Now in this vision he saw different types of angels and new instruments. The angels were arranged in ascending order based on their height and that of the instruments being played. He heard melodies which were simply tantalizing and divine. Melodies he had never heard before. He saw beautiful roads in a city that seemed endless. He even saw balloons and wondered if indeed heaven has balloons. In the midst of these melodies he heard the voice of God again clearly saying, 'In this day there is joy in heaven. My servant is coming home.'

He then woke up, pulled his pillow against the headboard to read the Bible. But even before he could open the Bible, he received a telephone call. It was Sarah's daughter...

"Mummy is no more!" she said, with a sob and tear in her eyes. McDonald immediately responded

'Praise God, she has gone home, her Father has called her. There is a beautiful place for her, God has shown me how beautiful the place is!'

The Funeral

McDonald then started assisting with funeral arrangements together with his church.

As it would turn out McDonald was given the task of preaching on Sarah's funeral. What amazed him was that at Sarah's funeral more than 300, people made a decision to make Jesus as their Lord and Savior that day including the village headman and the group village headman. And so, God used her passing to bring many into the kingdom of God.

After the funeral McDonald was approached by a woman who said she was blessed by the preaching. As she talked she indicated that Sarah was actually her cousin, McDonald thought the lady was rather extremely slender but since it was the first time to meet her, he thought nothing of it. As they talked the husband came over and greeted him as well. He then discovered that he actually knew the husband whose name was Mr. Chitsulo and he greeted them both with a smile of recognition.

Fast forward

Now 5 years later, in 2004 McDonald had a passionate ministry in the township of Ndirande in the city of Blantyre. He and his assistant pastors were passionately and faithfully praying for people and marvelous miraculous things were happening. The people they were praying for were actually getting healed and over time word got out of what was happening at their home. In fact, a few cancer cases where healed along with several other ailments.

The first person to be healed was a Mrs. Kamwendo who asked for prayer for the healing of cancer. The woman lived in Blantyre. Her husband heard testimonies of the healings that were taking place and called McDonald and his fellow pastors. He took them home to his wife where they prayed ardently for her and miraculously she was healed! The pain left her immediately and to ensure it was not some psychosomatic phenomenon she was asked to go for a hospital check-up. To the doctors' amazement, after all tests were done, there was no trace of cancer!

As if that was not enough, Mrs. Kamwendo called yet another friend of hers who also had cancer. This woman had a similar cancer problem to that of Sarah and immediately shivers went down McDonalds' spine. This was the same cancer that took someone close to him. Anyway, this woman was a civil servant and a teacher with limited resources to spare.

The Malawi hospitals visited so far, said they could not treat her case since at that time Malawi did not have adequate cancer facilities. Zimbabwe and Tanzania also said they could not do anything for her and also, that her illness had progressed terminally. She had been given early retirement and was unanimously sent home by all the hospitals she consulted.

To McDonald's amazement, the woman said she recognized him and that actually she had lost a cousin 5 years back to the same cancer and McDonald actually preached at her cousin's funeral. She was actually Mrs. Chitsulo and reminded him that she had introduced herself to him after Sarah's funeral. She had started suffering since that time and actually before that time. McDonald quickly remembered his observation of an unusually slender lady,

"*So it was the cancer*" he thought. A quick calculation of the time gone by did not do anything to ease the fears of the irreversibility of her condition.

"*God better come through for her otherwise she will die like Sarah*"

He thought

"*I hope I don't get embarrassed here*"

He whispered to himself in his mind, whispering as if anyone could hear his thoughts!

But in faith McDonald and his friends prayed and to his amazement the woman got healed! The pain left her and strength began to return. This better not be one of those psychosomatic healing where the mind tells the body to ignore the, pain. Yes he wanted her healed but its worse if she thinks she's healed and later regresses and stops believing in God. That would be awful! Both God's and my reputation were now on the line" he thought.

So like all straight up and honest ministers would do, he decided to follow the example of Jesus who subjected himself to human confirmation of his healings. Just as Jesus would send the blind and the lepers to the high priests, he also sent her back to the hospitals and to be examined. And examined she was, first skepticism as a live and ongoing case with at least a 5 year history, then with curiosity and wonder as to why the results where different from those of the past. Then to outright bewilderment as they pondered the impossibility of an error in their previous diagnoses and treatments. Because to the doctors' amazement they could find no trace of cancer and to McDonald's own amazement and relief.

Because God had come through for him.

"But wait a minute" he thought,

"It was not about me, God came through for his child!"

He marveled at the second healing of a type of cancer that had taken the life of his very own associate pastor way back in 2009. And above all, marveled at the sovereignty of God whereby he could heal one and not the other.

McDonald never met the Chitsulo's until March 2018, when he met the husband who testified that the wife is in perfect health and that shortly after the prayer his wife was reinstated to her job because her strength had returned!

So it was, that Sarah's death was not only grand and extremely divine. It even unleashed the miraculous and enabled others with her very own illness to get healed. O what a departure!

12

Mercy

The peacemaker

Mercy was a sister in law to my uncle, and my dad's elder brother. Hers is an interesting story. Mercy had been battling illness for several months and had been admitted in an out of hospital on two occasions. Now, in the month of February 2018, she was critically ill and was told by the doctors that there were little prospects of her recovery and that it is recommended that she undergoes home-based care. This would help her spend precious time with her loved ones in her final days.

She heeded the doctor's advice and was discharged from hospital as she continued taking her medication from home in the city of Lilongwe. While in the city she requested to go to her home village in Balaka and was ignored... much to her annoyance. She insisted and repeatedly asked that she needs to go to the village saying I have a great work to do in the village. Her sister wondered at her request as she mused at what type of work this sickly sister of hers had to do, "Could she even raise a broom in her state," she thought. Even more startling, she gave instructions to the family in the village that "please mill enough maize flour" because she would be receiving a lot of visitors, according to her.

Finally, everyone gave in and allowed her to go to the village, after all why agitate a terminally ill patient, who would want to further shorten her days with hypertension? No body want's that on their head, they thought.

She arrived, at the village on a Wednesday and immediately embarked on a personal mission. She called a string of 8 people with whom she wanted to make peace.

There was one person she was so angry at that at a time when she, Sarah herself, was sick in the hospital, she did not welcome this sister of hers with joy but instead with bitterness due to her anger stemming from a muddled history of a very, very poor relationship.

She was the first person to call,.. and said to her

'sister do you remember when you visited me in hospital I was so hostile to you and even asked you why you had come to visit me? Please forgive me for that'.

She also called her cousin with whom she was in bad books, and with whom she had not spoken for a very long time. She reached out to her and asked for reconciliation and forgiveness. When she met each of the 8 people, she would share a scripture and then sing hymns of worship with the person and would finally pray. What was startling was that she would not need a hymnbook. She would sing all the hymns by heart and the visitor would simply sing along.

She also called her son, who was a bit mischievous and quite the troublesome child. If you needed a solid example of a bad apple or black sheep, he was a striking image of that. She called him, telling him that she is about to die and tasked him, the black sheep with a responsibility, contrary to expectation, that on her funeral the family should gather and he should read to them Ephesians 4:25 to 30 and meditate on this scripture with his brothers in order to lead and direct their lives to resolve all strife in the family.

She specifically instructed him to repeat verse 29 when reading the passage. She also gave the family hymns to sing on her funeral and one of them was *'The Lord is my shepherd I shall not want'*. The scripture she left reads as follows:

'Wherefore putting away lying, speak every man truth with his neighbor: for we are members one of another. Be ye angry, and sin not: let not the sun go down upon your wrath: Neither give place to the devil. Let him that stole steal no more: but rather let him labor, working with his hands the thing which is good, that he may have to give to him that needeth. Let no corrupt communication/unwholesome talk proceed out of your mouth, but that which is good to the use of edifying, that it may minister grace unto the hearers. And grieve not the Holy Spirit of God, whereby ye are sealed unto the day of redemption.'
Ephesians 4:25-30

She was so concerned about the welfare and peace of her family that she reminded them that, above all, they are members of one another. They belong to each other and are essentially one, regardless of any differences they may have. Therefore in the midst of all disagreements though they be angry, they should not sin. In fact, they should mind their speech so they do not speak hurtful things and divisive words that break the family. They should instead seek to make peace and to speak things that build each other up.

By doing this, by living in forgiveness and in graciousness they will not grieve the Holy Spirit of God.

After her mission was done, her sister left her in the village to go back to the city to take more personal luggage as she had underestimated the length of time she would need to spend with Mercy. On the Sunday of the same week, she called Mercy to check up on her. She was surprised at the energy in Mercy's voice. She asked how she was doing and Mercy said this is a good day! I slept so well as if I am not even sick, I feel so at peace! I am so happy and feeling much better already, I even ate a lot. The energy and joy in her voice came from such a relational and reconciliational week and Esther realized that when Mercy said "I have a great work", she was referring to this work of reconciling with all her relatives.

The following Tuesday, Mercy spoke to her sister and Mercy said I am not too well today. It does not look like I will make it beyond today and I think I am going home today. She gave instructions on which songs to sing on her funeral and these were,

'The Lord is my shepherd' and 'nearer my God to thee.'

That day she sang a lot of hymns and read the word of God. One peculiar thing was that she was so keen on knowing the time. In the afternoon she kept on asking about the time. She was constantly asking *'What time is it?'*

And in the evening she asked and was told its 6pm. She continued asking until she was told its 9pm to which she responded

"Are you sure its 9pm? Because I want 3 am that's the time I am interested and concerned about".

She continued her inquisition late into the night until she was told that its 12:00am. She then got annoyed and complained to her guardians that they are lying to her since she has been asking about the time for quite a while now. Soon she was told that it was 2:30am she then had a twinkle in her eye and though immobile at the time, she demanded that they carry her to the living room so she could see the clock on the wall for herself. Her guardians were so perplexed and resorted to simply fetching the wall clock and bringing it to her. When she saw the time as indeed being 2:30 she said, "so you're telling the truth, my journey is now near'.

So, Mercy continued to chat with her relations that night until 3am. When it was exactly 3 pm she simply stopped talking. Her relatives continued chatting until they discovered that she had stopped talking. They all wondered why she stopped talking at 3 am thought perhaps she had slept. However, they decided to wait on her for 30 minutes until at 3:30 when they acknowledged that Mercy had actually stopped breathing and had indeed died. They were so confused because she did not show signs of death such as gasping for air or any discomfort among other things. She simply closed her eyes at her appointed time of death. Mercy the peacemaker, had transitioned to her eternal home!

13

Lenita My Grandma

The woman with a loving heart

Lenita was my grandmother on my dad's side and it so happened that a child in our village, where she resided, was orphaned. This child was a male child called Gershom ('Geresomu' in the vernacular).

All the relations called for a meeting to discuss how to care for Gershom and on who would raise him. In Africa, it is normal for family members to gather and decide on the wellbeing of orphaned children.

The culture is such that your nieces and nephews are as good as your own children and they automatically become your responsibility if your brother or sister passes on.

When asked who would keep him, one of his uncles said

"because he is a boy he will not be of much use around the house and if it were a girl at least I would have been able to give her chores around the house. I can't keep the boy".

Relative after relative gave reason after reason, and excuse after excuse for not taking Gershom in to their home until the family meeting ended.

Lenita heard of the predicament and decided to do something about it. She had two boys of her own, so another boy would not be too difficult to take care of. She talked to her husband and he agreed to the idea of adopting Gershom into their family.

On the morrow, she eagerly told the family that she will be able to take Gershom into their home. As my uncle explains it, Lenita was quite a caring mother and did not discriminate against Gershom, and raised him as her own. In fact, she took more care of him, than them so they thought! He tells of a story of how he, (Elias) and John were trained to take good care of their new brother. When she would give them cobs of maize (sweetcorn) she would call both of them and say share your corn with your baby brother. She would take the full cob of corn from Elias and break it into two and give half to Gershom, she would then do the same to John.

"At the end of the day Gershom would have a full cob of corn while we would only have half a cob" said my uncle Elias...

"So it would be with other food we were given. Gershom always had a lion's share!" He recounted.

Elias and John would also be taken to task whenever Gershom cried. My uncle Elias explains that one time Gershom was crying and immediately grandma Lenita called him and simply asked

"Why is little Gershom crying"

To this he answered

"I don't know".

Grandma then responded

"Ok is that so. Then please start crying yourself"

To this he answered

"Mum, how can I just start crying, can a person just cry without anyone hitting him?"

My uncle chuckled in hindsight and said

"Little did I know I was crucifying myself and claiming responsibility for causing my little brother Gershom to cry. She would later ask me to get my own whip and give me a good spanking. After this I would be told that little Gershom should not be crying and that I should leave him alone."

Anyway, a few years later a son was born to her and he was to be the last born of the family. When this son was only 3 months old, Lenita grew terribly ill. She had sores along her throat and could not eat any solid food due to the pain and swelling. She also had problems breathing and was generally in great pain. She was given medication but things did not improve.

After several weeks of battling this illness she became extremely weak due to lack of adequate nutrition. Later she fainted. Now in the village, people are very careful regarding how they handle fainting and, in case of apparent death, in the final hours of a person. They do not mourn someone's death if that person has simply fainted, to do so is taboo and to invite the actual death of the person. No one wants to be seen to be anticipating death.

So, some 30 minutes later the elders of the village came and examined Lenita. With no pulse, no breathing and with a deathly cold, they saw that Lenita had actually died. They deliberated amongst themselves and now another 30 minutes later they gave the verdict, Lenita was dead!

Then, only at that declaration, cries of weeping and mourning were heard from Lenita's house. Her body lay cold in the house, as the medical phenomenon called 'rigor mortis' set in, resulting in a stiffness of her limbs.

However, 2 hours after the verdict was given Lenita came back to life! Perplexed and astonished, everyone wondered what had just happened. Lenita soon explained her experience. She said

"I died and was met by 2 men dressed in white robes. The men were tall and sturdy. They told me that my time has come and that I will be taken by them. I then asked them,

'Ndiganeneko madando?' "May I please plead my case?"

They allowed me and I pleaded with them that 'what will happen to my 3 month old son?" One of the men said, "Don't worry about that because other people will raise him".

The other man then disputed and said "actually this lady is saying the truth because she likes children. You remember Gershom? She is the one that raised him so she really does have a genuine love for children"

The other man then said "I think you have a point" then he said "ok we have heard your plea and we have changed our mind. We will come some other day." After they said this, the men went away and I woke up" said Lenita.

What is even amazing is that my grandma Lenita Died in December 2016 at the more than ripe old age of 105 years and even I got to see her and relate to her as a grandson and son to my dad Jeffrey who was then only 3 months old!

When I think of Lenita, I think of all those who take care of the orphans and help the underprivileged. I am encouraged that God does not forget our good labor of love and that his reward is indeed ready for us. And that reward may just affect this life of ours on earth!

14

Ellen's Appointment

The woman who was on time!

This is a story of Ellen my aunt, who was my dad's sister. She had been sick for a while and this particular weekend her condition deteriorated significantly so much so that on a Friday evening all relatives were alerted of her terminally ill situation.

Because she lived in the village her 3 brothers living in town some 70 km and others 300 km away could only make the trip on the Saturday morning.

Her two brothers finally set off from Lilongwe on Saturday morning and they arrived at around 2pm. The other brother, Jeffrey, my dad, travelled from 300 km away and arrived a little later in the mid-afternoon.

Ellen was however more stable and managed to explain her ordeal. She explained that

"On Friday I was not well, I was visited by two men dressed in white robes, whom I knew were angels. They told me that they had come to take me and that my time was up. Later they told me that they had changed their minds and that they will come tomorrow on

Saturday. They said they will come at 6 o'clock. However they said "don't mix up the time, we're not coming at 6 o'clock in the morning but in the evening so get ready".

When my uncle heard this he thought these are the simple musings, hallucinations and babblings of a very sick person. After all she was not in possession of a wrist watch nor was a or

They prayed with her and soon they were joined by other visitors from church who also wanted to visit and encourage her. As they sang Ellen would stop them and say that's the wrong tune, in heaven that's not how they sing it. She explained that she could see heaven and that it was beautiful. She explained that she is going to heaven to her heavenly home.

Everyone looked at each other in bewilderment but they prayed with her and left.

So my uncle and his relations settled down and got a sense of relief that at least Ellen was stable and was able to talk. They were now getting ready for the evening meal and the food was being prepared. It is common for supper to be dished in the very early evening because of lack of electricity which forces people to have an early dinner and then to retire to bed. This gives more opportunities to not only rest but also be busy with other important though pleasant routines like obeying God's command to fill and conquer the earth.

Anyway, they were now quite comfortable and chatting away. Talking of the going-ons of the village and sharing warm stories of families in the village.

As they were about to start eating, they heard small sobs, coming from Ellen's house, they listened more carefully and the sobs turned into cries which grew into wailing. They looked at the time and it was just past the hour of 6 in the evening. This time she hadn't fainted, she gasped her last breath and stopped breathing.

They all recalled what she was saying about the angels coming again at 6pm and wondered at how wrong they were to dismiss her.

15

Wisdom

The musician who went out in song!

Wisdom was a friend and mentor to me. He was a man with many talents. He was an auditor and accountant, and was also passionate about music. I had an opportunity to work with him at one of the big 4 audit firms.

When I joined the firm I worked with him on my very first assignment which was the audit of an oil company, Exxon Mobil. I saw his passion for music grow over time and his specialty genre was Christian hip hop.

In time, he produced his first album which sold many copies across the country. He then produced several other albums including one album in which he celebrated the love of his beautiful wife called "Natchaisa" and later another album called "Linga Langa" meaning "fortress" or "God is my fortress".

As Wisdom's career grew, he was later sent on an international secondment program, to the USA and then on his return he left the firm and joined the industry. He continued to pursue his passion despite holding senior management positions in industry. However as his career and my own accounting career grew, Wisdom had a few health challenges and I was privileged to visit him and see how he was doing at the time.

In time, he continued to battle his ailment. There was a point in time where Wisdom was so thoughtful about all of his actions. I recall speaking at an internal auditor's conference in which Wisdom was there. I ended up talking about my time with Wisdom and how he impacted my life and how we worked together at a professional accounting firm on a "difficult" client.

Little did I know that Wisdom was concerned about my comments and asked me what I meant when talking of a "difficult" assignment. He thought for some reasons I was complaining about him during the time we worked together since the assignment was quite a 'complex one'.

"Far from it"

I said, and I explained that I cherished his mentorship and training and that the difficult work was indeed a challenge which made me develop as an accountant. It was shortly after this experience when I heard that Wisdom fell ill again, was admitted to hospital and even flown out of country as his situation took a turn for the worse. Later on into his illness, he died and his death was a shock to me, to his family, the nation and the music fraternity as a whole.

Soon, news started springing up regarding supernatural events surrounding his death. As Wisdom was battling his illness, he had divine experiences. The first experience is when Wisdom saw a King dressed in a white robe entering his hospital room. He looked around to his guardians and noticed that they remained unaware and consequently unaffected by this King's presence.

On one occasion, his mum was with him and he asked her if she could see this king. When the King appeared, he knew it was his Lord and savior Jesus Christ.

On another occasion, he saw the King walking into his room. He again asked his wife saying 'can you see King Jesus?'

And she said "no" she could not see any one in the room except for themselves.

This happened about 2 weeks before he died. And a week before he died he had another supernatural encounter. He told his wife he could hear sweet music being sang in heaven by children. He explained that the music was so beautiful and the keys and scales in which they were sang were unheard of,.. he had never experienced anything like that.

Now Wisdom was not only a musician but also a producer. And he produced high quality and well famed music. So for him to say the music he was hearing is outstanding means it was really supernatural and out of this world. He explained to his wife that he later asked Jesus if he could go there and sing along in the music.

Shortly after explaining this experience to his wife, Wisdom stopped talking and he later passed on in the following week.

Wisdom was a musician who had a divine encounter with God in the time before his passing, and not every person has pleasant or divine experiences like these that speak of the supernatural coming into the natural. He served God through song and God, likewise, welcomed him home in song!

16

Eddie

The guy who lived every day like his last!

It was that time of the year whereby as an audit firm we needed to recruit in preparation for the busy season ahead of us. It was that time when audit deadlines have to be met. So as is the normal practice, the two sets of interviews were set and I was on the panel of the second interview. There was one young chap who appealed to me so much. His name was Eddie.

When I interviewed him I found him to be quite a unique young man. The lad was not only smart but seemed to be well exposed, and had a well-rounded personality. He did not seem to only be as good as the books he was studying he seemed to have a broader perspective to life. He seemed to have other interests in addition to his studies that helped him develop into a leader in his own right. I asked this young chap what extra-curricular activities he was involved in and he gave me a mouthful. I then asked if he has learnt anything recently and he told me he had just read and been most impacted by the title "The Art of Leadership" by Dag Heward Mills in addition to other professional material he was researching.

I was greatly impressed with a young man whose interests are much broader than studies and also who demonstrates leadership at such a young age. A person who seemed extremely passionate and with a zest for life.

His energy was contagious and also exciting. Not mere zeal but with a touch of wisdom and maturity. As we decided on who to employ, I made sure to plead my case with the other panelists and finally I managed to convince them that we employ him. I even asked that if my colleagues were not convinced with my choice, I would be happy to have him work in my office where I can benefit from his energy and passion. So I prevailed! And it was settled, we were going to employ Eddie in our big four audit firm.

The contract was drawn and the phone was rang. We told the young gentleman we were happy to offer him a place in our firm. He was excited and elated with joy as were the others who were successful. I for one was so excited that I had found a promising accountant and a true diamond in the rough!

But it was still about 3 months before he could even report for duties since he had to finish his degree studies. As we waited for him and his colleagues to report for duties I heard some ear catching news! A student at a local university had drowned at the lake! On further enquiry, the university was the one we had recruited from, in fact the student was an accounting student. I thought nothing of it apart from normal compassion that such a young life would be snuffed out at an early age.

Shortly, the news started circulating on social media and it was accompanied by pictures. Ding! My phone rang. It was one of those many WhatsApp group messages so I ignored the messages. Later on, when I was a little free I looked at the message and the story of the drowned student had been shared. Sensational as usual it came with a picture. I looked at the picture and alas! It was actually Eddie!

My heart sank, I was thinking of the so much promise this you man had ahead of him. How could he drown weeks before graduating? What of his parents? What of their hopes for his bright future? What of their joy that their son had already secured a job before he even graduated? All these questions went unanswered. One day when I was with one of our church pastors at the time, Pastor David Kalilani, fondly called "Pastor D" by the youth. He was talking about Eddie.

Apparently he knew him closely. More closely than I, obviously. He brought a new perspective to Eddie 'story. But somehow after hearing his story, I finally felt a sense of peace.

Pastor D explained that he, as a youth pastor, had interacted with Eddie at the University. In fact, Eddie came to him explaining that he was the chairperson of a youth ministry called "Livewire". He explained that in the recent past he did not have this leadership responsibility and had received Jesus as his Lord and savior. He explained that now that he has an opportunity to lead, he wants to do something to impact his fellow students and to share his faith and create the opportunity for others to know Jesus in the way he knew Jesus. He wanted to do this through a music concert.

There was a sense of energy and also urgency regarding the request. Eddie further explained that he will give $420 from his savings which was almost all he had as a student. When Pastor D asked where he got the money, Evan's said he had been keeping his pocket money and he felt strongly that all of it be used for the "Livewire" revival on campus.

Pastor tried to probe further ensuring that Eddie knew what he was really doing, because he would need that money in industry for example for rental and household items and if not, then he would need it now for pocket money in school at least. But no! Eddie wouldn't listen! His mind was set on organizing an event at which people would be saved and enter the kingdom of God.

As they prepared for the event Eddie would visit Pastor D every week to share plans and tasks of what needs to be done. They started raising funds and it turned out that though people gave, Eddie gave the most in amount. I believe he gave the most in "heart and sacrifice" said pastor D, His heart was in the right place and his sacrifice was phenomenal for a student. The energy was high and the excitement was electric.

Now, as part of the preparations the organizing team including Eddie and Pastor D embarked on a prayer and fasting program. In one of the prayer sessions they sang the song "You are great, you do miracles so great there is no one else like you, there is no one else like you".

As they sang this song, God spoke to Pastor D saying

"Do you really believe that I am great? And that I can do great miracles? Or are you singing this song just for the sake of it?

If you truly believe that I am great I want you to make an altar call at the concert while you are ministering in song and to pray for the sick. Even if someone comes on a wheel chair I want you to pray for them and put your reputation and neck on the line for me, even if nothing happens at least you will have demonstrated that you believe I can do miracles and not just any miracles but truly great miracles."

Pastor David then told the people what the Lord had spoken to them and they prayed together.

On the day of the music concert, the sound system was set up and was crystal clear. There were various local artists that performed at the launch including Faith Mussa, KBG, Hola Music, Pastor D and others.

So as pastor David ministered in song he made the altar call in the midst of the song "you are great, you do miracles so great, there is no one else like you, there is no one else like you".

Immediately after the altar call there were droves and droves of young people lining up for prayer. As Pastor David and his team prayed for people. There was one lady who came for prayer, called Martina. She had suffered from asthma since birth. She came to the show with her cousin Tracy. Martina was someone who could not engage in rigorous physical activity and when she came to concerts she could not even dance because her asthma would be triggered.

But, after praying for her that night, she started dancing! Tracy got angry and asked why she was dancing, warning her that this would lead her straight to the hospital bed. But she said

"I am healed".

And she danced happily for the rest of the concert! That was proof enough to everyone in her family that she was really healed! But, there was more, when Martina was receiving prayer she had asked for prayer for her sister, Anna, who was at home. Anna was scheduled for surgery the following Monday and with the concert being on a Friday, she really had little time until the surgery.

Martina explained that her sister, Anna, could not eat any solid food because she had tumors in her stomach and she could only eat porridge. So that day Martina received prayer both for her and for her sister at home.

When she went home she found Anna eating "nsima or sadza, nshima, ugali or paap" (depending on which African country you're coming from) a local dish which was a proper solid food. In wonder and amazement Martina asked how it came about that her sister could eat solid food and Anna said I just feel like eating.

On the Monday the doctors prepped her for surgery. And before surgery the doctors checked her one more time before surgery. To their shock the doctors did not find any of the tumors that were previously showing on the abdominal scan. The doctors examined her again and concluded that there was no need of surgery because the young lady was healed. So just like that! The surgery was cancelled.

Tracy, Anna and Martina shared notes of what happened. Anna their elder sister was now so curious to know what happened with both of them and wanted to meet Pastor David, she said "sister I want to know the pastor who prayed for me and you the night of our healing.'

Anna received healing while she was distant and at home and, because of the sheer wonder of it all, decided that she must meet this pastor and followed her sister to Pastor David's church. Anna came to the pastor and explained that Martina had always wanted to join the pastor's church but that Anna had withheld her blessing and permission but from that day onward Martina was free to join the church. So Martina freely joined the church and is a member of that church till this very day!

So in Pastor David's words, "Eddie went with a bang! Because he sacrificially gave to an event at which people were healed, people gave their lives to Christ and others who had fallen back or backslidden re-dedicated their lives to Jesus Christ and many other people who needed counseling were encouraged. That is the way to go!" he said.

So here we have Eddie, a seeming tragedy, but in reality, had a short life of significant impact. He did what was important in life. He invested in the lives of other and had left an indelible mark on the lives impacted on the Livewire event that day. He had in-fact impacted generations to come because each life that was touched positively will have a positive impact on their own friends, family community and posterity. Eddie will surely shine like the stars in heaven because 'he who wins souls is wise and will shine like the stars' as it is written in the bible.

So for you and I, let's live our days like our last. Let's number our days and let's do what really counts in life!

17

Grace

A second lease of life!

Grace was a lovely soul. She had battled cancer for quite a while. And after months of fighting she knew it was time to tell her children what was to come.

So she called her son David (or Dave), her daughter Zorah and her niece Loreen. She broke the news that she had cancer and that it had now progressed to stage 4 cancer which is terminal. She explained that the doctors had given her only 3 months to live due to the seriousness of her illness.

But Dave, Zorah and Loreen where children of faith. They decided to stand together with their mum. They discussed what should be done and decided they would pray.

They decided that they would pray and fast and developed a weekly schedule where they would all physically meet and pray for their mum.

They started to pray and in the first few weeks it was emotionally hard to know that they are dealing with a sickness that is not only almost incurable but is already in a terminal stage. But still they prayed, and they prayed and they prayed. It seemed to them that they now knew the feeling of the Israelite army marching endlessly around the Jericho walls with no apparent breakthrough in sight. But still they chose to pray as they circled their own Jericho walls.

After several weeks of prayer, 12 weeks to be exact, it was time for Grace to travel for specialist medical attention in India. As the time came for her travel's her personal prayer team of Dave, Zorah and Loreen, continued to believe God and pray for the healing of their mother Grace. Grace eventually travelled to India and the doctors ran various tests on her.

With much anticipation she awaited the test results and the prognosis of her illness. To their delight and surprise they received the first piece of good news that the tumors that were in her brain have totally vanished and the tumors in her lungs and stomach had shrunk significantly.

To the delight of the praying trio, Grace lived an extra 3 years. She was given a new lease of life from 3 months to 3 years! Imagine that!

Grace's story does not end there, David explained that two weeks before his mum eventually died he started a bible study schedule with her. He would read the bible to her and they started reading the book of Luke and they would read part of a chapter or a chapter every day and they ended their study on Chapter 6 of Luke on the day she died.

What was very interesting though, is that on the day she died Dave managed to lead her in prayer and she received Jesus Christ as her Lord and Savior. He explains that on this day it was as if Grace saw her son for the first time. Dave was no longer the child whom she nursed as a toddler, no longer the one who needed caring for, no longer the young teenager but actually a servant of God who led her, his own mother, to Christ and faith in the atoning work of Jesus on the Cross of Calvary!

In fact, by this time David was now a pastor (fondly called "Pastor David" or "Pastor D" among young people) and even Zorah was now a pastor's wife.

That's why they stuck it out to pray for their mother hoping and trusting in God for the miraculous.

Other interesting events surrounding Grace's death were the various predictive messages they received as a family regarding the death of their mother. For example, Loreen dreamt that Grace was walking in a very dark corridor, surrounded in darkness but interestingly there was light in her footsteps so that wherever she set her foot on, shone, yes... each footstep shone and there was light everywhere on the path she was walking on. Dave's other sister, Linda, dreamt that Grace was in a cathedral called "St Michaels and All Angels" (a stately cathedral and national treasure in which I have been privileged to worship) and she saw her mom, Grace looking so young and beautiful, and that there was a big event happening on that day and at that event Grace was saying her goodbyes. She then later discovered that she was dreaming about Grace's farewell. In retrospect it was discovered by the family that in fact the funeral ceremony of their mum actually took place at that very same cathedral!

Dave's own experience just before Grace was re-admitted into hospital and before her demise was that he drove out of town and as he was on his way he met a storm with heavy rain and dark clouds. Dave could not really see where he was going as the visibility was extremely poor. But Dave felt God prompting him to press on and soon the storm cleared and the sun shone. He then felt God telling him that 'you will go through a rough patch but you will come out just fine and your mother will be in a better place'.

This was something he brushed aside because by then he was praying for her healing and not her demise.

So here is Grace, a lady who trusted God and was given a new lease of life! I am hopeful that whoever you are you can equally trust God and he will give you the grace to go farther than you ever hope for. Your 3 months can extend to 3 years and even extend to complete deliverance out of your troubling situation! So be encouraged, trust in him and see his deliverance and blessings in your life. And whatever storm you go through, press on because God is with you all the way!

18

Travis

The boy who died and survived...
Twice!

Sharon was expecting the birth of her son. They already knew it was a boy and as all couples do, they had discussed at length on what name to call their son. As usual, they would come up with a name and would think of another one, Sharon would come up with a name and Bill her husband would come up with another. Finally, they decided on one name and it was Travis. Now Bill and Sharon were Christians and they trusted on God for a successful delivery and birth of their darling Travis.

On the due date there was so much joy and expectation. The young couple went to the delivery room and the doctors started to give them the preparation they needed.

As the labor process started, and with much anticipation, the baby was born. But the nurses were too quiet. The atmosphere in the room soon turned to one of urgency and seemed to border on panic. And while other nurses attended to Sharon, others attended to the baby. The couple seemed confused as to what was going on. The nurses took the child expecting a baby's first cry but none came through. They gently slapped the baby on the back to trigger a cry but nothing happened.

Sharon looked at her husband Bill and asked what's wrong. Then they were told that their child was not showing signs of life. The baby was already born blue and it was now 10 minutes of trying to resuscitate him. But they still frantically tried to save him and then put him on an oxygen ventilator. Then they came to her and said there is nothing they could do.

But Sharon and Bill trusted in God, they prayed on the delivery bed crying out to God in the name of Jesus. Pleading the blood of Jesus over their child. After they said their prayer they heard a cry from the little baby. Doctors rushed to baby Travis to stabilize him and attend to him. And with joy they reported that they don't know what had just happened but finally managed to resuscitate a baby who was still born and who had already died in the womb.

But the prayerful and believing couple knew that what had happened is not natural but completely supernatural.... God had come through for them!

Later on in life, little Travis was now 4 years old, very intelligent and very social. He was in his bedroom one lovely morning somewhere in Germany playing his favorite video games.

After some time, the sun shone through his window and the sun rays were just beckoning him to appreciate the lovely morning .

So he went to his window to simply admire the day. The view from their 4th Floor apartment was serene. He could see the streets and down on the ground were some of his neighborhood friends playing in the nearby playground. He could hear the kids giggling and chasing each other on the peaceful day. In the playground below Travis saw some little girls playing. Then he noticed his good friend Tasha, the little girl from the neighborhood and immediately thought of saying hi.

So he opened the window and decided to sit on the window sill. But Travis being Travis, and the charmer he naturally was, decided to say hi to Tasha and her friends in style. So, true to form, he charmingly smiled and waved. With a smile on her face Tasha heartily received her warm greeting for the day.

As Travis extended his hand to wave, suddenly Tasha's smile disappeared into sheer terror. Something was not right.... Travis suddenly felt his legs flipping over and gravity taking its course... bewildered and disoriented Travis panicked. He could feel himself falling and all of a sudden his little 4 year old body fell crashing to the ground.

Travis's mother and father were in the house that morning when all of a sudden a little boy from the outside playground came rushing in. 'Travis is dead' he said and his mother looked at him in shock! His father immediately called out to him and shouted 'Travis!' Now the kids in the house had a funny culture. Whenever their mother called them they would not respond till the third time but when their dad called them, they would respond immediately.

So when Travis's Dad heard no response he knew something was wrong.... his mother immediately rushed to the bedroom where she had left him playing video games. She entered the bedroom and found an empty room. Hoping she had made a mistake, she quickly scanned the room but all she saw was an empty bed and the video games deserted.

Then she saw the curtain flapping as if beckoning her to come over to the window. She looked through the curtains and saw an open window and immediately knew something was seriously wrong. She went to the window, looked down and there on the pavement lay the body of her son Travis.

Her heart was now pounding and her brow now filled with sweat. She had to get to her son and took off, dashing down the 4 flights of stairs without even knowing it.

Meanwhile, Travis's Dad had already dashed out of the house and went to the pavement where his son's lifeless body lay. Immediately, someone reported the incident to the hospital that was luckily nearby and just across the playground. By this time a crowd had already gathered and covered the scene of the accident.

Everyone came to take a peek to see what happened and the nature of injuries sustained. News was now spreading fast in the neighborhood as the crowd frantically communicated with friends and relatives of what had just happened.

The doctors finally came after several minutes and found the lifeless little body of Travis. They examined Travis, assessing his injuries, he was covered in blood.... bleeding from his mouth and ears, his eyes rolled back from the shock of the impact with the ground, they were checking for a pulse and any sign of life but it was not there. The doctors turned to both his father and looked him in the eye. For a moment the doctor was speechless then he forced the words out of his mouth, shaking his head from side to side, he said 'I'm sorry he's gone... your son is dead'.

The doctor took off his white overcoat and used it to cover Travis's little body, waiting for emergency staff to take it to the morgue. He was then cordoning off the area and pushing the crowd back. Sharon and Bill, his mum and dad were also kept away from their son. But Sharon wouldn't settle for it. She pushed through the crowd as the doctor still held her back, saying that 'I'm sorry ma'am he's gone, he's gone!'

In spite of all this Sharon's motherly instinct kicked in, and it's in such times that a mother can do things beyond your imagination, times when they see their child in trouble.

She insisted and when a mother insists, well, you know.... So, extremely distraught, she shouted

'If he is dead then you can't harm a dead body, let me see my son!'

With that her husband stood by her and said to the doctors and police 'let her go' and fueled by her motherly love and passion she pushed through and they let her in to see her son. She picked up her son and carried him in her arms. Travis was covered in blood, his tongue was split in two! And she was also covered in his blood...She shouted 'Jesus!' and nothing happened, she cried out again 'Jesus!!' still nothing happened. Oh, but wait, just then something happened inside her. It was as if something rose up in her spirit, bubbling and billowing out! And with so much fervor she shouted again 'the blood of Jesus!' She shouted so strongly that the words billowed in the hearts of the on-looking crowd! And immediately she said that Travis coughed out the blood from his mouth. The doctors and emergency staff immediately attended to him and took him to the nearby hospital for more medical care.

Bill and Sharon were not far behind and they too rushed to hospital. When they got there they were told that 'sorry he's gone, the coughing was a reflex action that usually happens when a person finally dies and leaves his body, I'm sorry. He's gone'. But Sharon again would not settle for anything less than a living child. and she said if God wanted to take him, he would have taken him when he fell.'

She prayed and prayed, and the doctors still tried their level best to help him breathe. They hooked him up to life support machines and he was assigned to the Intensive Care Unit desperately trying to keep him alive. He stayed like that for the next 3 days with no signs of real life only in a vegetative state.

At some point they knew that the doctors would ask them to make that fateful decision. They would have to let him go and switch off those life support machines. But Sharon told the doctors that, "you have done all you could do and it's time for me to take my child home". The doctors said there is nothing more they could do, they could not allow her to take her child in his condition, there is nothing more they could do but wait.

Sharon kept telling them that if God wanted to take her son, he would have taken him when he fell,

"My God don't do a half done job!" she said.

So she knew to do what she knows best. And that is to pray! So she prayed to God, and she prayed to God, and within that same week the hospital called them saying there were changes in Travis' condition and that he actually woke up. That was as answer to her prayer. The doctors could not explain what had happened since all they were waiting for is to turn off his life support system. But Sharon knew that this was as a result of prayer and of a wonder working God!

Soon, they were discharged from hospital. But on the way home Travis said,

"Mom I need to tell you what happened"

Sharon said,

"No we can't talk about it coz the doctors said if you do, you could have a flash back and this could put you into shock and if this happens you may get into a comma again and may not come back to us."

But Travis said,

"No mom you have to hear what really happened."

Sharon became, curious and was afraid at the same time, but somehow, she thought it was really as if something else had happened, something rather mysterious because the energy in her son was off the charts.

So against the doctor's advice she allowed him to explain what happened and he said

'Mom, I started falling from the window but I never actually hit the ground! Because right before I hit the ground a man with a big hand caught me. I couldn't see his face because there was a bright light in his face.

The man asked me, "Do you want to go with your Mom or do you want to come home with me?" Little Travis wondered at this question 'do you want to come home with me?'

Which home was this? He thought, but instantly he discovered something, that he has another home. An eternal home where he will be with this man. He was careful to note that the man did not say 'do you want to go home with your mom?' Meaning that where he lived then was not his real home, it was in fact just a temporary shelter!

But as a little child, he was so close to his mom and was only getting to know her so he still needed to be with her for a little longer. So he made his choice and he answered

'I want to go with my mom'.

The man said

'Ok you can go with your mom but next time you will go home with me'.

Little Travis was curious to know who this man was. And thought how would he explain this to his mom? Who would he say he saw? Who would he say caught him from falling and hitting the ground? So Travis politely asked the man

'But sir... what is your name?'

To this the man graciously answered

'Son, my name is Jesus the son of the living God, the Great I am, and The Bright Morning Star!'

Sharon marveled at Travis's story and knew that it could only be God who saved her son. This boy had a bright future before him and he would later grow up to be a great musician and worship leader.

He even pastors a fast growing popular church and does a lot of world tours preaching the gospel in word and in song.

19

Esther

The Lady who set off on a long journey

It was a beautiful Saturday morning. The sky was blue and the sun was shining. Esther felt so blessed to have such a lovely and bright morning. She was a woman of faith. She had a faith in Jesus Christ as her Lord and Savior. She was a treasurer at her women's church group. She had a good sense of humor and was very sociable. She was the type of person who could get along with anyone and whose company you would naturally enjoy.

Around the house that morning were two of her nieces who came to visit. Her husband had left for town but the previous day she had announced that she was going on a long journey soon. Of course no one took her seriously since she was thought to simply be making jokes. This lovely morning she again repeated her statement to her sons saying,

'I have a long trip to embark on'

And still, everyone thought she is again just being as humorous as she normally was. To everyone's surprise she seemed rather busy and had a strange sense of urgency in her mind that morning'. Interestingly, she started packing her personal effects. Her husband, Bob, came back from town and found her busy packing.

He wondered what was happening because as a couple he knew of no such trip!

So, off she returned to the bedroom and continued packing.... she neatly packed all her clothes in suitcases and then tucked away all her possessions neatly in her bags.

Earrings bracelets, necklaces and all her jewelry. Afterwards she said 'I am packing because I am leaving' and I know that if I don't pack you guys can't pack my stuff for me, not as good as I have done anyway.'

And rhetorically she asked teasingly and jovially "can you guys ever pack for me when I am gone? You can't!" She said.

She then explained to her husband the financial situation of her women's church group. She explained that she had put everything in order and was ready to go on her trip. Bob was amused and curious thinking what on earth was happening to his beloved wife. She gave a full account of all the income and expenditure she incurred and any outstanding or unspent cash.

She explained how the reports were done where the files were kept and who should receive the reports and unused funds in her absence. Bob remained curious at what his wife was saying.

'Why the urgency? He wondered,

'Why do all these things now and not later?'

'Why pack all her clothes neatly and put them away?'

'Where was she going?'

What a mystery to everyone it was. So, this beautiful Saturday morning after Esther had packed all her things she started feeling rest-less. She went to the bedroom and slept on the bed. She then said,

'You know what? There isn't enough fresh air here. I need to be in a more open space'

So she went to the dining room. After just a few minutes she said the same thing.

'I feel out of breath I need to be in the lounge'.

Her two nieces said

"If you need to rest its better if you stay in the bedroom take a nap and rest a little".

Then she gave them some crude explanation of why she should not be in the bedroom. She then went to the lounge door just overlooking the verandah. She stood at the door and looked up as if focusing on someone or something in the far distance. Her nieces looked at her, she looked focused but more amazingly she looked so expectant with a glimmer in her eye. They asked her

"What are you looking for?" But she kept saying

"I am going on a long journey" and then they asked

"Are you waiting for anyone? What are you looking at?"

At this she turned towards them looked at them opened her mouth as if to say something then she held herself back. She looked at them again and just smiled. Then she looked up again and just stood at the door. Her nieces, Karen and Kate wondered what was going on.

After a little while, she stopped looking into the distance and said,

'Actually I now need to take a rest. I feel a little tired let me sit on the chair and take a nap'.

Karen and Kate still looked at her in surprise and wondered at all that she was saying, because the excuses she was giving to be in one place and not the other, did not make much sense. As they wondered what was going on, they knew deep in their minds that she was hiding something from them. They simply resigned to the fact that sometimes you have to respect elders since sometimes they may not be too comfortable to open up to you. So they let her sit on the chair. After all she looked more rested now. She was no longer looking into the distance and no longer preoccupied by anything outside the house. At least she can sleep and take a nap, rest and get refreshed.

Karen and Kate continued to chat about their girly stuff and they giggled away as they shared jokes and chatted.

They were there sitting with Esther on the lounge but then they thought something was a little weird. It looked like the couch were Esther sat in may not have been the best napping place especially for someone who was already complaining of not feeling so rested. They looked at her and thought 'she is definitely uncomfortable'. Her neck seemed too strained for her not to at least get an aching neck. So they decided the best was to move her to the bedroom again.

They knew it would not be easy since until now she really had not listened to them. But even if she doesn't agree, this time, they would convince her to, at least, use another pillow for her neck to be well supported. So Karen bolstered her courage and decided to wake her up and persuade her to lie down on her bed at least. So she politely approached her aunt Esther and asked her to move. Esther did not respond... and Karen had to call her again and wake her up. But she could not as before. She shook her and spoke to her without any response. She tried again and still nothing happened. Kate drew closer to see what was going on. Then she suggested to alert their uncle Bob. So they ran to him outside the house where he was.

'Uncle' they said... 'yes' said Bob, 'Auntie is not waking up' can you please check on her? Bob knew something was wrong. He rushed into the house, straight to the lounge where Esther was sleeping. He called out to her, touched her and saw that she was not responding. She looked like she was simply resting her head on the sofa while taking a nap. In fact she looked so rested and peaceful... except for the strained neck. But she did not feel as warm as she should be.

He checked for a pulse and he felt nothing. He checked for signs of breathing and there was none. Then he knew that Esther was not actually alive. She had passed on right there on the couch. Karen and Kate looked on to hear what Uncle Bob's assessment would be. Then Bob simply told them let's take her to the hospital your aunt is not well.

When they arrived at the hospital he told them the truth of what had happened but Karen and Kate could not believe their ears. They all recalled everything Esther was doing and saying that week. She was saying

"I am going on a journey. I need to pack my things, though I won't take my things but I know you can't pack them when I am gone"

She was going to the verandah looking into the distance as if waiting for an entourage, someone or some people. Then when the time came she simply sat on the chair and started off on her long awaited journey. She was privileged that she knew when she was going and, more importantly, where she was going. She was a woman of faith and she had set off on her personal journey.

20

Mike

The guy who knew he was going home

My cousin Mike was the adventurous type. I can describe him as jovial, always smiling and bold. He was quite outgoing and very street smart at the same time. He was also a growing believer in Jesus and he loved serving God.

Mike was quite talented and used to play several musical instruments. The bass guitar, the keyboard and drums. He loved to serve in the praise team by, not just playing instruments, but also singing, and over time wrote and sang a few songs of his own. Mostly, he would take the leadership role of the praise team. Part of this role would include wooing his fellow praise team members to practice and making sure they came, both on time and were all playing their part.

As he grew in passion and service, he also grew in adventure. In those days, and perhaps in these days too, there were stories of pursuing the African dream by moving to more stable and larger economies, and South Africa was a common and attractive destination.

His daring self made peace with this idea. But he first had to to tell his mom, since he had sibling sisters and needed to ensure that they are well taken care of in his absence. After all, he would be sending help to them so the family is supported. Soon he saved some money and got himself a passport.

The journey to South Africa is not the shortest, as it takes a couple of days of about 3 or so, depending on mode of travel and related fortunes along the way. However if it's by plane it is simply a 2 to 3 hour trip.

Mike made the trip by bus and finally settled. And his gift of music led him to join a local church where he continued serving God through music. As he continued his music, he used it to share the gospel and was later dubbed 'Evangelist Mike'.

He had such promise, and life was moving in the right direction. He later fell in love and found a life partner. They soon got married and settled together.

He was planning a trip to Malawi and his fellow musicians were excited to have him. They actually wanted to do a 'collabo' short for, collaboration. Now, before you start asking 'what kind of word is that?' Please note that that's their own slang not mine, as the narrator. This was a good plan, they thought, and would help him reconnect with his Malawian friends.

However, Mike soon fell ill and was diagnosed with a type of pulmonary pneumonia.

Just as he fell ill, he had a disagreement with his lovely wife, Thando, and it was so strong that she left him. So Mike was abandoned to recover on his own. Since he could not go to work due to his illness he eventually ran out of money. Soon he alerted his sister, Faith, in Malawi that he is not doing well but underscored that she should not tell their mom so she is not stressed.

'How are you mike?

'Not too good sis

'What's wrong?

'I am having chest pains

'I pray that you get better and how is my sister in law?

'She is not here, we had an argument and it's just me here

'Really?

'Yeah
'So who is taking care of you?
'I'll manage sis, I'll manage
'How long has it been?
'A number of days now, ..a number of days

He also needed some money and asked for anything Faith could muster up.

'I don't have much bro,
'Are you sure sis?
'Yeah, I'm not doing too good myself
'If you guys can't help me while I'm alive, how much more will you struggle with my funeral
'Don't speak like that Mike, don't speak like that
'I'm just saying sis, I'm just saying

After this chat, Faith got an eerie feeling and she immediately called her other sister Mphonyane, fondly called "Mpho" who was also living in South Africa.
'Hi Mpho, how are you doing?
'Hi sis, I'm doing fine and how about you?
'I'm fine thanks
'What's up?
'Mike is not feeling well and he is all alone, please go and check on him, he says he is having chest pains
'Ok, will do, and let you know.
As Mpho arrived she met Thando who had now calmed down and wanted to reconcile and 'come home'.
They found Mike in a 'sorry state', as Mpho puts it. He was almost skin and bones, and it looked like he was just starving himself. The house was a mess as everything was upside down with no one to clean and bring order and decency... and, he could barely walk.
Thando, needed to make peace and reconcile with her man.

'I'm sorry babe, I should not have left you and especially when you were sick, I'm so sorry for my outburst, I'm so sorry for leaving you and again I'm so sorry for abandoning you while you were sick. Please forgive me babe, please please forgive, I didn't know what I was doing, please forgive me, I beg you, please forgive me'

'It's ok babe, I guess I didn't do too good my self, If I had done better, I wouldn't have upset you as I did, I'm the one who should be apologizing not you' Mike said

They rushed him to hospital and discovered he had pulmonary pneumonia and that he had lost a whopping 30kgs!

His uncle and Dad visited him in hospital while his mom was in Malaŵi with the rest of the family.

Now Mike also had some issues with his Dad. Let's just say they had a "private altercation", so we don't open a can of worms here, and by the time Mike fell ill, it had been months before they had even talked. Mike knew he had to make peace with his Dad.

'Dad, please forgive me for causing you so much pain. I have not been the easiest son to have and I have caused you quite a bit of anxiety both in my earlier days and and now with my recent behavior. It's not becoming of a Christian and I am sorry, in fact now I believe you are my biological father and I'm so sorry for all the trouble I have caused you in my life'

'It's ok my son, I love you and don't worry about all that. Just focus on getting better.

'Thank you Dad, thank you and I love you too.

On one particular day, as his illness progressed, they saw that he was stabilizing and doing well. He was also in unusually high spirits.

That evening Mike asked his wife to call his mom in Malaŵi so he could talk to her, she called his sister Faith and asked to speak to their mom, when they gave Mike the phone he shared something simple but profound,

'Mom! How are you?

'I'm fine my son, my only son, how are you doing today?

'I am ok mom... but mom, I have achieved what God wanted me to do, and I will make it to heaven!

Not knowing what to make of her son's words she simply answered 'If that is the case my son, then it is well'

This was the last time Mike spoke to his mom, but she was at peace and thought he would get better without dwelling too much on what he was 'babbling'.

His dad and uncle visited again that day and as the visitation hour came to a close, they said their goodbyes and told him they will come again tomorrow morning, but Mike said

'Dad, you won't see me again tomorrow'

'Why is that Mike? Don't worry you are actually doing better now than the last few days so if you keep this up you'll be out of here in no time.

'No dad. You won't find me. I am going home.

'Yes you'll be discharged soon but I am sure we'll see you again tomorrow

'No dad, you don't understand. I'll be out of here indeed but I am not going home I am going to heaven

'Heaven?'

'Yes... heaven, in fact, my angels have already come to take me, they are just waiting for the appointed time, one is on the left side of my bed and the other on the right hand side. You won't find me tomorrow because I'll have gone home to heaven'

His dad was startled at this. Actually, he felt sorry for him because he thought he was really sick and perhaps he was "praying too much" at his church.

'Poor Mike', he thought,

'This born again business is causing him to babble strange things, but better to babble 'church things', than 'embarrassing scandals' he thought

'Bless his soul, But he'll get better' he told himself.

"He is more stable now, he is more stable'.

But, in the wee hours of that night, his dad got a phone call. It was from the hospital, Mike had passed on and he was no more.

Mike's dad, whom we call uncle Jonathan, remembered what Mike said and recalled that he was talking, with so much conviction, about 'going home', Yet he thought Mike was just losing it, and especially when he talked about the two angels. Now it dawned on him that he wasn't just babbling nonsense after all.

Mike's body was flown to Malaŵi and on arrival at the airport his sisters were heartbroken. He was the only son in the family and his sister Madalo (Meaning 'blessings') lamented the most,

'Oh my brother is gone!

Mike why are you gone?

Why have you left us all alone Mike?

Why Mike?

why?

Then, all of a sudden, she heard a clear voice talking back at her,

'Madalo, Madalo!

Kodi ukuona ngati mlongo wako utamupempha kuti abwererenso mthupi lake angalole?

Mike alikumwamba siyani kulira apa!'

Meaning,

'Madalo, Madalo!

Do you really think that if you can ask your brother to come back into his body he can accept?

Mike is in heaven and is safe, don't be heartbroken,.... just stop crying!'

When Madalo heard this voice she stopped crying in such a destitute manner, she was sobbing here and there but really would not cry with such hopelessness as before.

Among the eulogies was one from his friend that was expecting his trip to Malaŵi and it was a touching one. Because a few weeks earlier as he chatted with them, he spoke as if he is leaving South Africa 'for good'. This is what his friend said,

'Mike and I where planning his visit that once he comes over we will perform a collaborative song together. But he used to say don't worry my days of leaving and South Africa are soon approaching. I will no longer be staying here. That's all he would say.'

What was funny for his friend was that Mike was settled in South Africa and seemed to be doing fine. Also, he was building a new family that started with his new found love, Thando. He was also never talking of immediate plans to relocate to Malawi, so for him 'he will leave South Africa for good' was surprising. And when he heard of Mike's passing those words kept ringing in his mind. It came to him that his answer was not really the appropriate one but was rather diplomatic, if not cryptic.

'When are you visiting? Remember when you visit we should do a song together'

'Don't worry, I will be out of South Africa for good, and I will be going home soon, my days of being in South Africa are coming to an end' he would say.

If Mike didn't know that he would be dying at the time, perhaps it was God talking to, and through him, but surely in hospital he knew it much clearer and was less cryptic when talking to his Dad.

Everyone said Mike was gone too soon. He had such promise and plans to serve God. He used to preach the gospel as a young evangelist but God took him home too soon.

The local Malawian sayings were common at his funeral,

'we loved him but God loved him more'.

'Wafa ali mwana, he has died young, he has died a youngster

In fact his, tombstone unveiling ceremony was done on the same day as that of my other cousin Thoko, whose story is also told in this book. His friends who had served with him, lamented that they wanted to sing 'with him' and not 'for him' at his funeral and that they wanted to see him come 'walking on his own' and not see him 'carried in a casket'.

But, both the funeral and the tombstone unveiling (or remembrance ceremony) were infused with a spirit of praise and worship as dozens of his friends came over from his former Malawian church, the choir and his own praise team. They celebrated his life and his service to

God. And somehow the spirit of evangelism was also celebrated. And especially on the remembrance, as it was on this day that his aunt Elsie gave a testimony of her own son's salvation. And as we celebrated the life of 'Evangelist Mike' and the souls he brought to God's kingdom, we also celebrated the life of another precious soul, 'Thoko'.

So, here we were, saddened by the loss of two young lives. But the mystery of it all, and why they passed on so young is shrouded in the love of God. For Thoko, God needed to take him at this young age for his own good. But for Mike... it dawned on me that 'he was home'. And can you really ever go home too early?

He had served God and had something to show for his life, he was a worshiper and evangelist. And, like most parents who give curfews to their kids just to love them and enjoy their presence when they are back home, their kids can never be 'too early' if their dads and mums simply want to enjoy their presence. And, the younger their children are, the earlier their curfew is.

Maybe it's just me, but for Mike, it dawned on me that you can never be too early to come home. And especially if you have finished your assignment and that home is heaven, and God, your Heavenly Father, has determined your curfew'.

21

Mizeck

The guy who had a second a chance

A rich heritage

Mizeck had a rich family heritage. In fact, his great grandmother was the one who received the first missionaries of the Dutch Reformed Church (DRC) into his country, Malawi, which is fondly called the "Warm heart of Africa".

The word of God was not far from him ("mau samamutalikira" if literally translated from the Chichewa language) and he grew up knowing it. His great great Grandmother, just to humor you was actually inspired in the early 1930's by a Ghanaian missionary called Dr. Aggrey. Now, Dr. Aggrey was a learned African who was also a missionary of the DRC and he went about setting up missions and inspiring Africans to improve their lives as part of the church's strategy to bring civilization, Christianity and commerce. So she was inspired, and welcomed the missionaries to set up the local Presbyterian Church in the central region of Malawi. The church thrives until today and is one of the largest mainstream churches in the country.

This being said, this rich heritage was passed down 4 generations to the life of Mizeck. He could not escape its effect so that from an early age he knew the word of God! They used to pray every day in their home and the word of God became a part of him. Naturally, he realized the importance of receiving Jesus Christ as Lord and savior, and this, at a very young age.

He soon committed his life to and received Jesus as Lord and savior at the tender age of 14. As he progressed in his faith, life equally progressed. He went to secondary school called Dedza secondary school. This school was renowned for its quality education. It was set on a hill like a beacon of hope to the nation. And a beacon of hope it was, since it usually enrolled only the best and the brightest of students.

However, being set on a hill, it was a very very cold and windy place to be. And the town in which the school was is naturally mountainous and cold as well. So Mizeck found himself at this school and used to participate in the Christian fellowship of students called the Student Christian Organization of Malawi ("SCOM" or the "SCO"). However, as he interacted with his schoolmates he found new friends, friends who were not so good an influence. Friends who somehow drove him from the right path he had chosen.

He was in a phase in which he was being influenced by peer pressure and tended to please his friends than have a mind of his own. This led him to compromise his faith in Jesus. However, in an attempt to please his new friends he decided to be doing what they were doing, so he naturally got into some mischief! He was abusing alcohol, was involved with the ladies. All these were happening at a time he ought to concentrate on his studies and grow in his faith. But the good thing was, at least he could pray. He went to SCOM and even went to church. So he was actually acknowledged as 'still standing' in the Lord... but deep down, he knew from how high he had fallen!

His death

SCOM used to have evening prayers on certain days of the week where they would share the word of God. One particular night Mizeck wanted to get into his hardworking routine of studying in the dead of night because that's when he concentrated the most. But to do that, he had to sleep early. So off he went to his room. But his friend Ben, from SCOM came over. All energized and pious, he said 'Mizeck let's go for prayers tonight at SCOM...we have bible study!'

But looking at his workload he answered

'Sorry I can't, I want to study tonight so I must sleep early! Sorry dude! But next time will do'.

Disappointed at his response, Ben grudgingly went back leaving Mizeck alone. Mizeck immediately tucked himself into bed and pulled over the blankets over his face..... to keep out the cold of course. It was an extremely cold evening that day and for an African country temperatures of 5 degrees Celsius during the day or evening were not child's play. "In fact, these SCOM guys must be out of their minds!" He thought, how can they pray when It's so cold. After all, had he not needed to study he would have been using this time to chat and play chess with his friends, rather than use it for bible study. So he thought why would he battle the cold when he could rather be snug and warm in his comfortable bed? Which was only comfy by boarding school standards of course!

So he rested his head and savored the warmth of his blankets as he slowly dozed off. Suddenly he discovered he felt a bit of heat in his chest. He tried to figure out what was going on but before he knew it he could not breathe. Trying as much as he could, he tried to pull in air and then to exhale but he could not. He panicked but there was nothing he could do. Somehow he could not move his hands..... He sensed danger, great danger, he felt entangled and that something was covering his nose and mouth! But almost instantly, he felt the heat in his chest die down to a calm and he no longer struggled.

And,... strangely enough he no longer breathed either! "That's bizarre" he thought to himself! Suddenly he saw himself levitating and floating upwards... he was being separated from his body as if his body was a simple glove being pulled from his hand. He tried as much as he could to hold on to his body, but alas! he could not. It was as if something was pulling him away forcefully. And, try as much as he could, there was nothing he could do to stop himself!

He finally 'detached' from his body and floated about 1 meter (3 feet) above his body. Thinking perhaps he will drop back to his body he, rather unfortunately, levitated higher and higher. Horizontally he levitated to the ceiling. Then he knew he was done for! And he started to complain to God,

"Why would you take me like this? I could have understood if I had fallen sick or if I was involved in an accident at least I would know I am dying. But in my sleep? Why would you do that God?" He said... then he heard a voice saying

'look down at your body...' then he turned and looked and what a sight he saw! His head was entangled in his bed sheets and blankets! He was totally entangled and his hands were also wrapped up. Then it dawned on him that he must have suffocated and had indeed died! In an instant he saw every little detail about his dormitory, he could see all the cups and all the books and even every single spoon in the room. So he knew and accepted that he had died. But once he accepted that he had died immediately he started moving.

Hell bound

He moved so high up in the sky that he could see the details of his school and saw the school's shining lights fade away in the horizon just like you see a building fade away in the window of a plane or a bus as you drive away from the city and you look back on it. When he was explaining this to me in his own words he said 'We travelled at an extremely and insanely high speed and we were going very very far. But in only 3 seconds we arrived where we were going. I could sense that I was with someone or some force that propelled and carried me forward.' (For those Star Wars fans, like me, the author, it felt like a hyperspace jump but much much faster!)

Mizeck landed in a short moment in a new place. It was on land but it seemed like a different world or planet altogether. He then started walking on a path and just 5 meters in front of him he saw the path branch into two roads. One to the right and one to left. But Mizeck was not a novice to the word of God. He knew that in Christianity these two paths are talked about and he knew that he better not go to the left or that would be the end of him.

So he chose to go to the right. But try all he could, he could not advance forward. He felt like a little insect who is trying to walk through a glass window or a bird thinking it could fly through a glass window. Though he could not see any barrier, he was sure to his very core that there was something there and he could not penetrate it! But he could see from a distance that the place he was unable to go to has indescribable beauty, indescribable light and indescribable peace. In fact he could sense the peace, he said he could feel it and he could even smell it!

But he soon came to the realization that there was no chance of ever walking on that road! He needed to find another route. Grudgingly and unwillingly he took one step to the left. The moment he did that he felt a strong and irresistible pull that was propelling him forward. After 15 meters he felt the way close behind him after every step he took. Immediately he walked into a thick darkness that can only be described as a blackness. This was a darkness so thick that he could feel it and it cloaked him all around.

As he moved forward it was as if he was walking through a black substance a cloak and blanket that he literally had to walk through. He could feel it all over him... on his hands as he moved along and on his legs and he could feel it close behind him!

Mizeck said 'the moment I walked into the darkness I knew that everything had gone completely wrong!!' He felt the feeling he would get when all hope is lost, the feeling when a kid is about to cry but is telling himself not to cry and yet just making it worse, yes he felt it! That day he knew the meaning of the word 'despair'.

He felt regret and he felt guilt. He said 'I knew I had missed my salvation, and these feelings of despair and regret are so intense like you can never imagine! I could feel this in every cell of my body but a million times more. In fact if we were to feel like that on earth we would literally die! That's when I knew that every cell is really a living being, I could feel everything including my hairs and my toes. I remembered my biology class that said the human body is a combination of millions of living cells and could feel every cell on its own and alive on its own! I heard every cell complain to me saying

'Where are you taking us? We were obeying you when we were on earth but you are now taking us to destruction?'"

Demonic assault

So as Mizeck advanced forward he smelt something extremely foul! "It's a smell of death that literally sucks the life out of you. If it were to be smelt on this earth it would definitely kill with devastating effect. You just cannot live!" He said. Then he heard cries and screams in the distance.

At this point "I went mad" he said "when you hear that people can go mad, I went completely mad! And the feeling of despair was so intense!' When this happened, engulfed in the foul smell that covered him like a dark cloud, two demons appeared. One of them started reasoning with him and asking him why God created him. It said God knew that he would end up in hell. Why was he created if he would end up in hell? The other demon told him to curse God saying

'We too were angels in heaven why did he create us? We never chose to be created!'

But in the midst of this emotional assault Mizeck fell to his knees, kneeling in prayer! The demons threatened to beat him up and asked what he was doing. He said

"I want to pray for one last time that indeed God's word was true and it was me who did not obey his word".

Then Mizeck prayed..... and he prayed. With all his heart he prayed and with all his voice he prayed. He said,

"I have never prayed as fervently as I prayed that day! Thanking God for the very last time because I knew that from this point forward I would be in eternal agony and would not at all be able to pray to God!'

A strange man

But while Mizeck prayed, all of a sudden the demonic shrieks and cries stopped and there was a different atmosphere and a different presence around him. All of a sudden he felt an overwhelming and empowering feeling of love! Instantly all the despair left him and as intensely as he felt the pain of despair he also felt intense love and overwhelming peace.

He then knew that at least something must be going right for once! Because there is no way he could feel such love and peace in such a terrible place like this. Before he could open his eyes he felt a touch! A hand touched him on his shoulder and a voice called his name!

"Mizeck" the voice said,

"What are doing?"

"I am praying for the last time' he answered

"But don't you know that this does not work here? Why would you pray when you know that once a person is dead he does not go back to life? Didn't you know or hear about the Word of God while on earth?'

 To this he replied,

"I knew the word of God, I am praying to thank him for that word and to acknowledge that it was just my fault that I did not take heed to it'

So the man told him

'Stand up'

And then

'Come with me.'

Mizeck followed the man and they headed back from where he had come as he previously battled the dreaded darkness of this wretched place. And as they walked back they talked and chatted but one thing that Mizeck felt was extreme love. The love was so overwhelming and nothing like we feel on earth. Here we say we love each other but in heaven the love is so amazing, so pure and so divine!

Mizeck explains that

"As we walked the man I was with said 'ok I want to hear your case and see what you would give as reason for me to consider sending you back to earth and giving you a second chance' ".

So they got at the crossroads were he first saw the two roads one to the left and one to the right. He explained that "We had just come from the road to the left which was the road to hell. He then took me through the road to the right where I had previously failed to go. This was only the second thing that made me marvel at this man's authority, first it was retrieving and rescuing me from hell and destruction and the powerful and hideous demons, secondly it was giving me access to the righteous path. As we walked along this road the beauty of this place was literally 'out of this world' and the peace in this place could literally be 'smelt and felt'. We approached a golden pearly gate which was so very high in height. The gate was so strong and so heavy but as we approached the gate opened on its own. Inside the gates was a great number of angels.

The angels surprisingly were positioned behind the gate and along the road. Some were in the middle of the road and they all looked mighty and, honestly, fearsome. But as we approached, these angels made way for us and simply moved away. Some to the right and some to the left. The posture of these fearsome angels intrigued me. It was extremely respectful to the man I was with, in their might they gave honor and respect to this man. It dawned on me that I was really walking with someone with great authority! And this, more so, because the angels were staring at me intensely. It looked like their job was to keep me out and I could almost sense them saying 'you don't belong here!' Now I understood why I could not penetrate the path to the right when I wanted to. It must have been because of these fearsome dudes. I knew that if I were not with this man, firstly I would not have been rescued from the highway to hell and, secondly, I would not have been allowed to be in heaven."

A court hearing

Finally, Mizeck came to a room that almost looked like a courtroom and he was asked to argue his case.

"Why should we send you back" they said.

Mizeck knew that whatever he says better be good, and, most importantly, not self-incriminating! So he thought of something to say and thought he should simply say 'send me back because I was praying'. He knew that if he says 'I was a born again Christian' he would be caught out because he was living the best of both worlds and mixing his faith with sin and worldliness. On hearing his subtle response the man and his angels said. 'Aha! You have answered well! You were praying? So you know the word of God not so?'

To this Mizeck thought "but there are many words in the Bible" and if he said yes he would surely be caught out also. So he hesitated. Then the man said don't worry we will remind you of the words you heard while on earth'. After this they set him up to see how he lived his life. He thought he would watch it on a screen but instead he says they actually "rewound" him and he "relived" his life again. There was a specific moment whereby he had heard the word of God being preached when he was 15 years old. As he listened to the preaching he said to himself 'this preaching is really helpful. I will be doing what has been preached in order to go to heaven' at this the man said,,

'You see on this day you committed yourself to follow God's word so let's see where you applied this word'.

Then they fast forwarded Mizeck's life all the way to the time he died and found out that there was no where he applied that word or followed his commitment. He relived every life experience in the presence of this man and at the end of the day he had nothing to complain about because everyone could see all the sins he committed. They looked for areas where the word of God had an impact on his life but found none.

They gave him another chance to look at his life again and then a third chance then asked him what he had to say to defend himself or, if they have missed anything, for him to point out for himself where he thinks he used and followed God's word. He refused because he knew he would just implicate himself further. Then they gave him one last chance to defend himself and he took it. He then argued and said

'God, how can you take me like that? I was so strong and you did not give me a chance to know I was dying. Had I been sick or been in an accident I would have had a chance to repent but I was just taken in my sleep with no warning at all! Since you are a kind God you should have at least given me some warning of my death!'

Then they asked him how much time he thought he needed. He felt that he did not have much leverage in this argument and before answering felt so frustrated that he may actually be sent back to hell. He thought

'Why have these people taken me from that road to hell only to trouble me like this in an argument I cannot win?'

Immediately he thought these thoughts they asked him,

'Why are you thinking like that? Why do you think we are just troubling you and have brought you here for no reason?'

He was now afraid of just thinking carelessly before these guys because of what they said to him.

So before he answered the question of how much time he needed he thought to himself perhaps a week would do, but he then hesitated and thought

'if I say one week these guys will bring it down to less than that, they will definitely find something to say, so perhaps if I said one month I can buy myself a week!'

Then immediately the man said

'What if we gave you a week? Would that be enough? How would you have used our warning?' and he said

'Yes if I had a month I would have changed my ways!' But they told him that 1 month is too much but even though, we still gave you a month's notice, then he said three weeks but they told him it's still too much time, then he said 2 weeks until they brought him down to 1 week. Because, they said, they gave him enough notice in that month and he did not take notice.

He then argued the same way Abraham argued for the deliverance of the cities of Sodom and Gomorrah until he came down to 3 days then to 2 days then to 1 day and they still told him he was given all that time to prepare even until 5 minutes before his death. To this he marveled and asked how come he did not know of the warnings. But they told him that

'By the time you were going to bed someone was asking you to go to the students' fellowship for a bible study. Immediately you refused you went to sleep so you had our warning till the very very last minute of your life! So tell us where we should send you, to hell where we took you from or to paradise?'

Mizeck thought to himself 'but I have already failed all the tests and even if I say I want to be in paradise you people can't even allow me there'

He did not say this out loud but only thought it in his heart then they rebuked him saying

'Why are you thinking like that? Don't you know that you sons of men are foolish and not wise? Especially those without Jesus who do not accept God's plan of salvation through forgiveness in his son Jesus Christ! Don't you know that hell was not prepared for man but for Satan and his angels? You sons of men just get the punishment of hell by following Satan and getting involved in things that don't concern you because what Satan did in heaven by rebelling against God was none of your business but God has promised that he will punish Satan and all who follow him!

Hell was not meant for man at all because hell fire is too intense for man! In fact if God were to punish men he would simply punish them as he did to them in the days of Noah whereby he simply punished them with the flood and started again.' At this rebuke every cell in Mizeck's body felt so much hurt and regret, and so much guilt. As he recounted his story to me, he said

'Moffat, I have never felt like that before and it's like someone rebuking you but feeling the remorse and guilt a million times more intensely' he said he felt regret and helplessness because he knew that he would be sent to hell. He cried in despair knowing all hope was lost! He cried pleading for mercy and for a second chance because he knew that as he was coming to this place he had already seen his dead body, suffocated and lying helpless on his hostel bed.

But, in the midst of the crying he again felt a touch on his shoulder saying

'If you were to be given a chance what would you do differently?'

Then a glimmer of hope shone in his eyes, and he remembered the evidence of this man's authority as he had seen, then he thought to himself

'This man seems to have authority in all domains, on earth in hell and even in heaven. His authority snatched me from the torment of the demons of hell and even allowed me to come to this place when at first I could not do it on my own! Even when I am here these mighty angels who were blocking me from coming here were saluting him and making way for him'

Then he knew that if there is anyone who could send him back and give him a second chance it's this person. So he chose to take him at his word and believed him as the only chance he's got. Not just the only chance, but the only true chance! Therefore he took it and promised that he would change! He would repent of his sins, ask Jesus to be Lord and Savior of His life, and really live a life that pleases God! Of course in an attempt to save his soul he promised many other things such as, he would preach God's word and serve God all the days of his life! Amongst other things!

Then, against all odds, beyond all hope he was told,

'Alright I will give you another chance!'

Mizeck felt a great sense of peace, it was as if he was dreaming... how could this be? Men are usually given only one chance at life and not two. He left earth looking at his dead body and now he is being given another chance? Such grace and such mercy! He could not believe his ears. A great sense of peace overwhelmed him.

The trip back

Then the man took him back and walked him out of heaven to the crossroads. Now, from the crossroads to the place he first landed was about 5 meters. The man told him

"You can go back now"

But Mizeck was afraid thinking that he may again be sucked into the path to hell. But the man said to him

'Don't be afraid, it is I who is sending you back so you don't need to be afraid. How have you managed to come back from hell and into heaven and back again? You should have faith and go back by faith'.

But Mizeck was so scared of hell that he did not budge! Not a single step was taken! To this the man answered

"Ok if you won't go then all you will be left with is my voice which will guide you so it's better you try now because if you fail you can always call me."

Mizeck knew that he better listen because if he is left alone then it probably won't be good and he will have no protection from hell and he wasn't willing to take that chance either. It was too big a risk, and he was not willing to take. So he ran back to the point he landed and when looked back he could not see the man again and all he could hear was his voice. The moment he reached his landing point he immediately started to fall. He fell so fast and rapidly that he saw the planets and stars zoom past him.

It was another hyperspace jump! And he could now see himself heading straight for impact with his body that was lying down below. He fell directly into his body but his fall was broken by a certain force and as he made contact with his body it was as if he was supernaturally slowed down but he still felt a certain impact in between his lungs and on the area overlapping his heart. He immediately regained his five senses and all of a sudden could feel that something had covered his face.

He remembered how he saw himself and knew that he was completely entangled. He decided to roll to the side in the hopes of untangling himself. As he struggled to get himself free his friends surrounded him and helped him to get free. They could hear him gasping for air and shouting for help. The hostel was now full and his bed totally surrounded.

There was a multitude of questions directed to him. Was it witchcraft? How did you get entangled? What happened? But Mizeck was so confused and all he could say was

'I'm ok, don't worry, I'm ok'

He was so overwhelmed by his experience that he could not even start to explain himself to them. After all, how would they believe such a crazy story? How and wherefrom would he start explaining?

His experience had so much of an impact on his life that the very next day he asked, on his own, to go for bible study. Soon he re-dedicated his life to Jesus Christ as Lord and savior. He continued steadfastly in his faith and by the time he graduated he was still holding on to his faith.

By the time I was speaking to him he was a co-worker of mine in the same student's ministry (SCOM) specifically the ministry that is for alumni's of the student's ministry.

And, all in all, Mizeck is living a life of purpose that impacts the lives of many young people in Malawi. He is mentoring young people in how to attain success by acquiring life skills, academic excellence and career guidance and he is also sharing his faith in Jesus Christ with the young people so they too can live a meaningful life. I guess he is really fulfilling his promise to serve God and follow him. That time Mizeck was only in his teens but now he is in his late forties and is looking forward to his fifties. This is Mizeck the guy who was given a second chance of life and that.... against all odds and against all hope! Mizeck was literally saved from the very jaws of hell!

When I read this story I sometimes laugh at how Jesus almost tricked him into leaving heaven when he froze at the crossroads. Mizeck wanted Jesus to be with him all the way but Jesus knew his word alone would be enough. Then Jesus scared him into being alone and remaining only with his word. Too scared to go to hell and only remain with His word alone he bolted back to earth. Looking back to Jesus, Jesus was nowhere to be seen. I bet Jesus was laughing and though Mizeck was fearful, Jesus knew that his word was all he needed. Cool trick Lord. You have a divine sense of humor.

22

Shadreck

The minister who saw heaven

The early years

Shadreck the evangelist, was a well-known minister in Malawi. He is now gone to be with the Lord, but has left an indelible mark on his nation. He is someone you can truly describe as a person who 'served his generation'. He was an evangelist who preached the gospel of Jesus Christ, of salvation in his name and through his death on the cross of Calvary. His reach was multi generational and across all sectors of his society, and even across boarders.

His beginnings, however, were humble and just the same as for every other person. He was a church goer, water baptized and had a good relationship with his church. He was even serving in the church but did not really have a personal relationship with God. Shadreck was born on 29 October 1940 to a Christian family whose parents were church elders in the same church. He didn't do much school he only went to 4th grade in those days when Nyasaland (Malawi's colonial name) had not yet obtained independence from British colonial rule. So he could read English but could not fluently speak the language. Therefore even in his later ministry days he could only preach in the vernacular language called "Chichewa".

As he lived his life, he became a landscaper and outdoor caretaker in the government departments and was overseeing a department of caretakers for the surroundings of government buildings. One day as he was going home after dealing with the normal business of the day he was riding his bike as he normally did.

A tragic encounter

It was a Tuesday afternoon, on 28 November 1967. As he was turning at a T-junction he suddenly heard a heart piercing, very loud screeching sound, and turning to see what it was he saw in the corner of his eye a vehicle approaching and heading straight towards him. This vehicle, on his right side did not obey the stop sign. He panicked and struggled to decide what to do, 'should he brake or try to peddle harder and escape the vehicle?' Or should he just try to evade it? He only had a split second to decide.... But as he was thinking of what to do, everything went black... the car had ran into him already! And onlookers heard a bone crunching sound and a bang as the car tried desperately to stop, but all to no avail!

Instantly, things went dark, and Shadreck found himself in a different place. Looking around he saw a big white throne. There was a majestic being on the throne and he looked like a humongous man. He clearly had authority and he immediately knew this throne was a throne of Judgment. The man opened a great book before him and told him that 'according to your works you have been brought here to be judged!' He then said 'by the works that are recorded in this book you are judged and condemned to eternal punishment in the lake of fire.'

Immediately he said this, Shadreck started moving towards hell. He could hear the cries of people and their eerie, ear-piercing screams. The sounds were getting louder and louder and immediately he was filled with feelings of guilt and regret. Here he was.... a senior church elder, a giver in the church and someone who was approved and accepted as an established Christian, but, before God, he was a sinner. As he approached the gates of hell he saw a whirlwind in front of him. The whirlwind came over him and engulfed him! He thought it was the end of him..... Not knowing it is was new lease of life. He immediately resuscitated and saw a crowd around him. The crowd was startled at his resuscitation because it was now a full 90 minutes since he had been ran over.

By know the police had already come to the accident scene and had pronounced him dead. However though 90 minutes is a long time it was not unusual for a least developed country in the early sixties with no formal emergency response services.

The police marveled that he came to! They used their own vehicle and took him to hospital. Shadreck was in the hospital for a week and a half before he was discharged as fit for home.

A *divine encounter*

When he arrived home he had a vision. It was as if he was dreaming but then it was happening in the spirit. He heard a voice saying 'Shadreck you are not living the life worthy of a Christian. Someone who is a church elder should not be doing the things you do'.

Now Shadreck had a few vices in his life that you may not know about. Firstly he was passionate about getting rich. So much so that he had actually visited a witchdoctor to get charms to become rich. He was taken by the witchdoctor to a shrine in the graveyard where they performed some rituals and offered sacrifices. He was however shocked to meet other prominent people who had also come to get charms for their businesses. He was also a smoker and was addicted to cigarettes and the voice told him that

'all these things are not worthy of the life of a Christian leader'.

He should not be consulting with doctors and should not be visiting the grave to perform dark rituals. He was also shown a clear white screen and cloud of smoke. The screen became completely blackened by the smoke and he was told that 'man was not made to smoke, you are destroying your body'.

The other of his vices, more of an extension of the first, was reliance on charms for protection. The witchdoctor had given him a charm that would protect him from wizards and all forms of black magic spells that may be cast upon him. And whenever he was in a public place he was able to know who and who were witches and wizards and they would realize that he has found them out and he would then be 'left alone'. Their dark arts and spells would not work on him no matter how powerful the wizard was, so he believed.

Now the voice showed him what was really in the charm. Immediately he saw a spirit being, a mighty beast in the form of a lion inside the charm. The voice said many people are bound by sin and you are also bound but you will become free because of the blood of Jesus.

Shadreck was told to destroy the charm but he struggled so much to do that. It took him one week to get rid of it. Every day he would throw away the charm but would take it back, he would do this every day taking it back until the last day when he decided to throw it away for good without looking where it would fall so he does not know where to look for it.

And true to form after throwing it away he was tempted to look for it. He actually did look for it and discovered that it would be a futile exercise. That's how he finally got rid of his charm. Three days after he did this, the Lord Jesus Christ appeared to him and this was the beginning of divine bible school and many other visitations that would follow. He was taught what true Christianity is. That it is a relationship with Jesus that it is not 'working' for salvation and being 'commended' by men or by the church. He learned that it is about being washed by the blood of Jesus and therefore being delivered from sin and all the vices that trouble you. It is being accepted by God and not just by man. That it is also about living worthy of the new life and about the forgiveness given by Jesus Christ.

For Shadreck this was the beginning of a divine ministry. He would always preach what he was taught from heaven and all his sermons where by divine interpretation of the Bible and his continuous encounters with Jesus all through his life.

Serving God

From 1967 he continued to preach the Good news of Jesus to all manner of people. His message was pure and his message was divine. He was accepted by all congregations and all cultures and he was a mouthpiece of heaven! I (the author) was also privileged to be born in Christian family and in fact my father was also involved in a lot of church evangelism and had on many occasions invited Evangelist Shadreck to their revival meetings. He would be there on some evangelistic meetings as long as he was one of the organizers.

On some occasions Shadreck would be invited and would come with a colleague called Mr. Wells Sakala. Wells himself is an accomplished Evangelist and has done many a preaching in many a Church. The rest of this story is a story that was told in one of these meetings and recounted to me first by my dad and then by Mr. Wells Sakala many years later.

Zambian crusade

Now retired from the University of Malawi, Bunda College of Agriculture, Evangelist Wells recounted their Zambia experience and he was kind enough to welcome me into his home to explain how things unfolded.

Now Shadreck, was a minister who had a profound impact on Wells' life because he was a sincere man and a one whose works matched his preaching. This is something that is so rare in today's world since we see a lot of preachers and prophets, and ministers, whose way of life is quite contrary to their profession of faith. He later became so renowned that he was now preaching in several neighboring countries.

On this particular occasion he was invited to Zambia and his trip was well publicized. Evangelist Wells accompanied him as he usually did, more as a personal aide and comrade in arms, than a co evangelist. The meeting in Zambia was to happen in a medium sized stadium which ended up being filled to capacity.

Their host was a well-to-do Zambian business man and he welcomed them into his beautiful house. They were given a large room which had two beds at their disposal. He would later discover, however, that sharing a room with this heavily anointed evangelist was quite a 'dangerous thing'.

On the day of their arrival they talked and chatted and got to know their host who was so hospitable that they talked up to 10pm after which they decided to retire. They prayed an evening prayer and retired to their room. Shortly after they slept, and just after 12 am something happened and the spiritual gifting of God kicked in and started operating.

As Wells would discover, Shadreck had a gift of knowledge and revelation and God showed Shadreck a vision. In that vision both Shadreck and Wells had a large field to cultivate. They planted corn and it sprouted and germinated well. As it grew however there was a dry spell with no rain and a harsh sun. So much so that the corn wilted and was at risk of dying. Downcast and depressed they looked at each other and wondered whether or not they would lose their crop.

They pondered on what to do, and as they pondered, dark clouds gathered with thunder billowing away and lightning flashing, laden with rain. They looked at each other and wondered 'could it be that we won't lose the crop'... as they thought of this, a heavy and rich rain broke forth and watered the corn! The rain restored the crop and it did much better than before the dry spell, leading to a bountiful and hearty harvest!

After the vision, Shadreck immediately woke up and shouted
"Wells..."
panting and frantic he shook Wells endlessly shouting
'Wells wake up!
Wake up Wells!
Wake up!'

But, sound asleep, Wells took some time to respond and recover from his deep sleep. Unrelenting, Shadreck continued to shake Wells until he was wide awake.

'What did God show you, tell me what did you see? Did you see it? Did you see it?"

Shadreck shouted! Confused and bewildered, and barely lucid.....

'I saw nothing' Wells grunted! At which Shadreck recounted his vision to him and remarked...

'I don't know what God is up to tomorrow but I know it will be something great! God will shower his blessing on his people, I can feel it in my bones! God is up to something!' Please Wells... please pray let's pray for God to show up tomorrow because I can sense that this is what he wants to do'.

So they prayed and slept. But, as they enjoyed their sleep the same thing happened.

Wells was shaken rigorously again. '

"What did you see? What did you see?' Shadreck asked and again he replied 'I saw nothing'.

This happened for a third time and this time Wells, though indeed a man of God, was now quite irritated. He even thought to himself "why is God only showing visions to him and not me?"

But, barely an hour later, something happened again and this time... well let's just say 'Wells did not need any waking up!'... and it was Wells who rushed to wake up Shadreck who was now in tears and crying out aloud, not even restraining himself. He was all teary, sweaty and wet. Wells could hear him shout incessantly,

'Let me in, let me in please, oh just let me in, I want to get in now please let me get in!'

As Wells narrated this part of the story, shivers ran down my spine and my heart almost sank. I had heard too many stories of supposedly holy men of God who had missed the mark and had been denied entry into heaven! Hearing what Shadreck was shouting, "Let me in" spoke volumes to me. It shouwed that this esteemed evangelist was pleading with God to be granted entry into heaven.

Wells was so afraid at was happening. Evangelist Shadreck was not a young man. At his advanced age a person would not just cry anyhow! So he shook him on his bed and asked,

'Agogo (grandpa! Grandpa!)

What's going on!

What is it?

What is wrong with you Agogo?'

But the more he shook him, the more he cried, and the more he shouted 'let me in, let me in please, oh just let me get in, I want to get in now please let me in!'

Mwansa, their host was immediately concerned and disturbed. He ran from his bedroom in the far side of the house. Wondering if his guests had been attacked. He didn't knock on the door... he banged on the door! He banged so loudly that Wells thought he was literally breaking the door! Wells opened and immediately Mwansa asked "what is going on?" Clueless as to what was going on Wells simply showed him the crying Evangelist. The shouting continued and the host asked 'is he epileptic? Does he have some type of mental illness?'

"No" wells said, "this has never happen before!"

He shook him some more, and he finally came to, Shadreck was almost gasping for air now and panting heavily. Teary and sweating all over, his pajamas drenched in sweat, and eyes red with tears! He looked like he was worn out... as if he was struggling or fighting with someone. Taking a very deep breath he said 'Wells please give me some water' he said, actually he was now shouting, 'I need cold water!'

Mwansa rushed to the fridge and brought a bottle of almost ice cold water! Shadreck poured the water on himself and drank the little that was left. On hearing this, my curiosity was aroused. Was this man of God in some type of fiery torment in his vision? Any way the story continued to be narrated to me...

"What's wrong?" they asked him to which he replied 'Wells please pray!!!' Startled at this request... Wells and Mwansa looked at each and Wells responded 'but what will I pray for? I haven't seen what you saw", and he absolutely refused to pray.

Shadreck then explained his ordeal. He said 'I will never stop preaching the gospel, I will never stop telling people about Jesus Christ and his gift of salvation by his death on the Cross!! I was taken to heaven and someone took my hand and asked me 'Are you Shadreck Jonas?' And when I said yes he took me and said "come and see, let me show you the house you are building in heaven". As they walked they passed through beautiful green grass with very tall trees. They walked and the man talked. As he talked Shadreck's heart was filled with joy indescribable! And he wondered who this person was that brought him such unspeakable joy! He looked to his face but every time he did so the man turned his face away. He did this so many times that he simply gave up trying and so he decided to look at other areas of this man's body. He saw his hands and saw that they were scarred and nail pierced. And immediately alarm bells rang in his head. 'Isn't this Jesus?' He thought to himself? Then he decided to look at his feet and saw world renowned features 'oh it is Jesus!" he said to himself "it is Jesus!' he has nail pierced scars on his feet.

Then they came to a large mansion. 'The house', Shadreck said, 'was indescribable. the foundation was as clear as glass, and the foundation was so very deep!'

He started describing the house but could not, and as he tried to describe it he started crying again, the more he tried to describe the house the more he cried! Until after a few minutes of recollecting himself he started again...... The gates of the mansion were pearl and had an inscription on it of his name 'Shadreck Jonas' as they approached it the gate automatically opened for them, he could now see the house. Decorated with shiny and precious stones. He saw the house looking somehow transparent but at the same time opaque. It was made of precious glass and decorated with rubies, emeralds, and jasper. He tried to describe the type of house and failed to describe it. He started to cry again because he could not find the words and could not believe that God was building such a beautiful house for him in heaven. As the gate opened for him he saw this absolute marvel of a mansion! A house that was so luxurious, and shining, and twinkling'.

At the sight of the mansion Shadreck wanted to get into it and started going through the gate. But, Jesus told him,

"this is the house you are building with your service to God. But you can't go in now because you're work is not done! So do not stop preaching the message of salvation!"

On hearing this a struggle began because Shadreck wanted to enter his house immediately! The more he tried to enter the gate the more Jesus pushed him back. And the more he struggled the more he cried and said

'Let me in, let me in please, oh just let me in, I want to get in now please, let me get in'

Everything now made sense to Wells and Mwansa. Then Shadreck said

"We should never stop preaching the gospel of Jesus. Each one of us is building our house in heaven and the foundation of our home is receiving Jesus Christ, and the building materials are the good works we do for him. That's why 1 Cor 9:2 says 'no eye has seen, no ear has heard, the precious things that God has prepared for those that love him',

'I cannot describe what I saw. I cannot describe the peace that I felt! The peace is so overwhelming and so different from that on earth. I really want to go there' he said with his eyes welling up again with tears.

'I was crying because Jesus was telling me it's not time to go into my house and it's not time-to go to heaven. I am really sad because I want to go to heaven!'

Finally, my heart was at rest! Here I was, fearing for the worst, and thinking that Evangelist Shadreck was being warned by God for missing the mark and that despite pleading with God to let him into heaven he was not eligible to do so. All unbeknownst to me that actually heaven was too good for him to wait. Heaven was a place he wanted to go to and a place he was willing to wrestle God for! Wow! I was blown away! Is heaven that good! You bet it's that good!

Based on the testimony of the beauty and peace, and authority, and the deep infusing love of God, it is too much of a magnet for the true believer to continue considering clinging on to dear life because dear life is not so dear anymore. Dear life pales in comparison to the brilliance and intensity of heaven. No wonder Christians whose stories I had heard of thus far, seemed to always transition almost willingly and mostly expectantly of receiving this great and awesome place.

No wonder Paul called this body a 'tent'... 'a cloak' that can be put off when it is no longer useful. No wonder it's referred to as simply being a container! And perhaps that's why Apostle Paul said "For me to live is Christ and to die is gain"

I now understood the struggle that Apostle Paul had between almost "choosing" to "live" or "eternally benefit from dying" when he said,

"If I am to go on living in the body, this will mean fruitful labor for me. Yet what shall I choose? I do not know! I am torn between the two: I desire to depart and be with Christ, which is better by far; but it is more necessary for you that I remain in the body. Convinced of this, I know that I will remain, and I will continue with all of you for your progress and joy in the faith," 2 Phil 1:21.

It seemed that Paul had overcome the urge to transition to heaven because he had a task which he called "fruitful labor". Shadreck on the other hand had experienced this for the first time and it took God himself to convince him that his work on earth was not yet done!

Wow! This literally blew my mind away! But by now my musings had sidetracked me. I needed to continue listening to Wells as he finished narrating this profound story ....

So, then their discussion automatically turned into an early morning, if not midnight, bible study as they then focused on 1 Cor 3:10 - 15 in which Paul says,

"I have built the foundation and others are building on it but they should take care how they build because their work will be tested with fire and those whose work is tested and survives will receive a reward'.

Shadreck then said it's ok to receive Jesus as Lord and savior but it's even better to serve him and do good deeds. Because if you have an opportunity to serve God and do not do so, it is a shameful thing and a lost opportunity because there will be a differentiation in heaven! He reminded Wells and Mwansa of 1 Cor 15: 58 which says that whatever you do for God is not in vain. He emphasized that you are going to be paid and well rewarded by God and also that while those that receive Jesus will be saved and go to heaven it is those that serve God and those who win souls for Christ who will shine like stars in heaven!

So whatever opportunity you have, please make it a point to serve God! Because even in the classroom there are distinctions, there are some who get a bare pass, some who pass with credit and even others who pass with distinction!! Our aim should be to enter heaven and hear the words 'well done good and faithful servant you have been faithful with the very little you had!' "

When I heard this, I felt in my heart that Shadreck had now accepted the importance of him being "put out" of heaven for now. He had indeed understood that serving God is fruitful labor and indeed that "it is more necessary for the world that he remains in the body."

As Wells recounted this amazing story to me, he told me that this is why he still preaches about Jesus and that is why he still serves God! He said he wants to serve God when he still has the chance and while it is still day because night is coming when we may not have the chance to serve him. So my own word of advice is "whatever good thing you find to do for Jesus do it with all your heart!"

23

Adam

A touch of resurrection power!

A victim of stigma

Adam Usi Phiri was born in the Zambian Copper belt and had Malawian parents, Ali and Janet, hailing from Mangochi in Makanjira. He was born prematurely,.. due to social pressures on his parents. Well, what I mean here is that they had just given birth to a baby girl, now a few months old, and to have another child within 12 months would be a big taboo and source of shame in the community. So even though the pregnancy was far along fortunately it was not very prominent and they decided to abort their baby at 7 months.

Little thought was given to the life growing within Janet's womb. After all, when does life start they thought? They subscribed to the idea that it only starts on birth and not within the womb. After all, the baby was just a fetus with no rights and really had no life. Ali told Janet she had a right to do with her body what she felt fit. They would then seek out local abortion herbs commonly used to poison the fetus within her and trigger the violent contractions that would literally destroy the little life growing inside of her and expel its lifeless body in a pseudo delivery.

As fate would have it the abortion ended up being a violently induced birth leading to a prematurely born live baby instead of the poisoned fetus or mangled remains that ought to have been simply, or not so simply, disposed of. And so Adam was born and born alive! And stayed 2 months in an incubator from 15 June to 15 August 1967.

Unfortunately the poisonous effects of the herbs affected Janet's womb leading to an infection that would take her own life in November of that year. However, baby Adam survived and lived on milk formula provided by his father.

Finding and losing God

At the age of 13 in 1980 Adam received Jesus Christ as his Lord and savior. He continued in his faith in Jesus until the age of 16 when his father discovered about it. He called him and said "Adam where we come from in Malawi we are Muslims and even your grandfather is a Sheikh at the mosque. So as your father I forbid you from practicing Christianity and you should become a Muslim from this day forward." His father demanded to meet Adam's pastor and when the two met it was a clash of faiths. The pastor explained why Adam had believed in Jesus while his father explained why he should be a Muslim. At the end of their discussion they respectfully agreed to disagree and as a father of the child he exercised his right to forbid his child from following Christianity. Adam therefore joined Islam and was immediately circumcised at the age of 16 and sent to Madras so he could learn Arabic and more about his Muslim faith.

As Adam unfolded his story to me, he explained that his family returned to Malawi in 1999 and in 2002 Adam started dealing in drugs such as cocaine, mandrax and in precious stones and also the side hustle in fake precious stones. "In short I was thief!" he said. He became reckless with alcohol and started womanizing and ended up contracting HIV and Tuberculosis. He was put on medication but by the time this happened his body had already deteriorated. By the time he started his TB medication he had already lost so much weight and said

"I was already almost a skeleton and the strength of the medication only worsened the situation for me, I only took the medication for 2 months, but by that time I lost even more weight and was reduced to bone. I could no longer walk and they always had to carry me. It was not too difficult to carry me because even though I was a grown man and very tall, I weighed only 27Kgs".

On 24 July, as Agnes, Adam's wife, explained, Adam woke up in good spirits. She was excited that he even had an appetite that day. With a pretty good day she started preparing a meal for him that evening at around 5pm. Evelyn, her mother in law (an elder sister to Adam's late mum) was also around to visit and she helped tend to Adam. As Adam was waiting for his food at around 6pm he started feeling paralysis in his toes. Slowly the feeling crept up to his angles and then to his knees and thighs. Then he knew he was dying.

"As the paralysis moved up I could feel my inner man, my spirit, being pushed upwards" he told me. He then called for all his family; wife, children and father and some other relatives and started telling them that he is dying. All the time he repeatedly prayed in Arabic

"Ī allah 'akbar! "Ī allah 'akbar " meaning "God is great! God is great". Agnes was so afraid that she and his father called for the sheikh to pray for him. Unfortunately he was not home and they called another sheikh from another mosque and he came quickly with some herbs and said some prayers. But the paralysis continued until it reached his chest and even his neck. Immediately, he said, he heard a sound "whoosh" as his spirit was pushed out of his mouth and he heard another sound "click" in his throat as if something was closing behind him. Then a voice in his ear said "Adam if you hear that there is death ....this is death".

Immediately, in the twinkling of an eye Adam found himself landing in another world, he flew and landed as if he had wings and found himself on a small path surrounded by beautiful grass, very green with beautiful flowers.

Meanwhile on earth Agnes had gone back to the kitchen to collect the food she had been preparing thinking that it would give him strength to her now babbling husband.

They would eat together so that his spirits are lifted with people around him. She rushed to the kitchen and as she sent her son to deliver the food to the bedroom, Evelyn sent him back. Agness, could not understand why, but she sent him back to deliver the food again and again Evelyn sent him back....and this time Evelyn asked for a bucket of water.

Agnes brought the bucket of water and they poured it on Adam in an attempt to resuscitate him thinking he has, perhaps, fainted. By this time all the prayers had been said by the sheikh but to no avail. They accepted he had died and then started sending messages of the tragic news to their loved ones and the whole village and people started wailing as a sign of the death that had just occurred. All the neighbors gathered and, in true African fashion, stood with them in the night vigil as they mourned their loss.

Meanwhile Adam continued on the path he had landed on. The path was paved with beautiful terrazzo-like stone with beautiful gems and precious stones that were glittering in front of him. He immediately felt an immense sense of guilt and said to himself

"What will I say for the things I was doing on earth?" He said he just knew that he was guilty and no one had to tell him that. He followed that path but ahead of him was a cloud of fog which seemed to come and go and constantly change form. As he approached the fog, he immediately found himself on a very broad road. He could not understand how he had moved because he was now in the very middle of the broad road and he could see both ends of the road on his left and his right.

A community is startled

Then he heard a voice,

"Adam, Adam! What you were doing on earth was sinful and today you are going to hell".

As the words were spoken the ground on which he stood shook

violently. When he heard the words "hell" he fell to his knees and touching he knees there was a wind that blew over him and immediately the sense of guilt and fear left him. He immediately said to himself in his heart

"What God has judged, he has judged".

He decided not to move from where he was on the road so he could see whoever would come along the road to take him to his punishment in hell. As he waited he said to himself

"But God aren't you able to forgive me, please have mercy on me oh God?"

Then he heard a voice

"Adam! Adam! I have forgiven you. Go back to the world and tell them that I am the only one God! And tell my people that there is a lake of fire that is eternal, go and be a preacher and do not get employment for I shall feed you myself. Pray for the sick, for I have given you power to lay hands and heal the sick and go and take care of the orphans'.

Immediately this was spoken, he heard the sound of birds singing and chirping. It dawned on him that he was now back in his body. It was now almost 5 am on 25 July but he could only see darkness and discovered that his face was covered with a cloth because he had died. He pushed away the sheet and sat up. He looked around him and, as African tradition would have it, the mourners had already filled his house and surrounded him in his bedroom wailing loudly as they mourned him. He immediately spoke and told them that "Stop crying God has sent me back." And everyone cried some more not in sorrow but in fear and confusion!

At this point, Agnes explains the atmosphere in the room better,.. She was petrified as was everyone else.

"I wondered at what had happened. I heard Adam speak strange things about God. I did not know what this was about and feared that it was not my husband talking but perhaps a demon. I feared for my life that if this is a demon speaking he would become violent and possibly harm us. I decided to run away from the bedroom and go to the living room" she said.

Immediately, everyone in the room ran away and followed her until there was no one in the room.

Once the room was empty Adam heard the voice audibly speak to him again,

"Adam! Adam! I am God and I am Holy! I don't mix with anything evil, take out everything that is here!" Adam knew what this meant. He had now relied too much on witchdoctors and charms. He had some of these charms in his amulets, and pockets and even some medication in his body lotion. He then went to his shelf and took all the cocaine, the mandrax, the charms and all bottles of medication. Agnes had now entered his room and he gave all these things to her.

"I simply hid the lotion because I thought Adam was still 'out of it' and threw away the rest'. Agnes told me.

Adam heard the voice again saying "Adam, take off your pajamas in which you died and wear new clothes"

So he asked his wife to bring him knew clothes and he took them and wore them on his own. Agnes then asked about the bottles of lotion saying "Are you sure I should throw the lotion away"

To her it was a waste of expensive lotion and a hole in their budget.

"Yes, haven't you thrown it away already? There is some witchdoctor's medicine in the lotion" So on hearing this she took the lotion and threw it away.

When Agnes left the room the voice spoke again and said

"Now Adam touch yourself to witness the power I have given you, to heal the sick. As you heal the sick, you too need to experience this healing power."

Adam then felt his weak and, now bony, hands rise up almost as if someone is lifting them and touched his head. Immediately he felt like a surge of electricity was flowing through his body.

Electricity, and heat, and power, flowed through his hands onto his head and from his head all the way to his toes. He wanted to remove his hands but could not. The hands moved downwards as if under the control of another person, perhaps the person that was speaking to him. He touched his chest. Then his stomach which had been extremely bloated due to his long illness. At this point the swollen and heavily bloated stomach experienced miraculous healing. He could not understand why but the hands started pressing his stomach inwards.

All of a sudden it literally shrank and could hear a sound as if air was flowing out of him the same way a basketball would be deflated when it is so full of air. As the power moved downwards through him he was told to touch his legs and immediately power flowed through him and he felt another surge of power. He then felt so much strength in his legs and body. He stood up and a looked at himself in wonder and amazement. He again heard the voice saying

"All the people who were crying for you are still around in the living room, go to them".

Adam then went to the living and stood on the living room door from the corridor. He saw the people who were now too confused and afraid. Confused enough to leave the bedroom but afraid enough not to leave the household and be seen as deserters. He then said to them "You people are you running away from me? Why are you afraid of me?" The first person to answer was Adam's father who said "But Adam you were dead" Immediately he said this Adam saw a flash of lighting in the room and he could supernaturally see the hearts of everyone in the room. He saw the common heart shape we use nowadays "but it was aligned as if with LED lights just as you see on a Christmas tree" he said.

"The lights flashed and I could immediately see the condition of the hearts I was looking at. Stubborn hearts, rebellious hearts and adamant hearts and I was shocked and said 'God are people's unforgiven hearts like this? So stubborn and hard? Please take me back because you have already forgiven me I should not deal with such hard hearts Oh Lord' ".

Then Adam started going back to his bedroom.... to die... yes he wanted to die! Now that I think of it, it's quite interesting. Did he think God had resurrected him only for him to despair and give up? So what was he expecting? To lie down on the bed and die at will this time? Anyway, as fate would have it God would stop him in his tracks. Immediately he heard the voice again "Adam, Adam go back and pick your father" Immediately as if someone was forcing him he went to his father grabbed him with his hands and lifted him up suspending him in midair for a minute. He then he put him down. Then the voice said "go and lift up your aunt Alinemba" as he moved to words her she screamed in fear "No no no! Please don't touch me" fearing for her life from this skeleton that was approaching her. But Adam grabbed her and suspended her in midair too.

After some continued shouting and protests, he put her down. He then heard a man's loud sobs that turned into crying. Turning to his left he saw his father who was now in tears. He then said

"Adam I have now truly believed that there is God. A skeleton like you, who was unable to walk and had to be carried everywhere! How can you carry heavy people like us? I believe that there is God and you can do whatever God has told you to do and I will never stop you again."

Adam continued narrating his story to me and said that "Then the voice said to me 'Adam start the path you took when you were 13 years old, that is the true way' this is what is said in John 14:6 in which Jesus says 'I am the way the truth and the life. No one comes to the father but through me'

You just gotta love women

He then told his father that 'the way you stopped me from following when I was 13 years old is what I have been told to follow" His father told him he was free to follow the instruction that God has given him. Meanwhile his wife thought the medication had made Adam delirious. So she insisted that he be taken to the hospital. They drove him to the clinic in called Area 25 Clinic and told the doctor what had happened. At this Adam explained his ordeal and the doctor said "I know the people who are mad or delirious but he is very coherent in whatever he is saying so I can only provide him with medication to let him rest and sleep but I see no problem with him'.

When they came back home Adam was already asleep because of the sleep medication he was given but once he woke up he continued telling his family about what he had experienced in heaven. His father told him that he would like to follow the path God had showed him and that day his father and all his family made a confession of faith in Jesus Christ. They all received Jesus as their Lord and savior and they follow him to this very day.

Reconning with spiritual folly

However, in 2007, Adam had a relapse of TB and decided to stop taking his antiretroviral therapy... because of his faith in God. After all, God had anointed him, sent him back from the grave and even healed him, he thought. Once he did this, his CD4 count dropped to the count of 40 and was admitted to hospital again and, was at risk of dying. It took several elderly Christian pastors to counsel and advise him that he should still take his medication until the doctors certify that he is HIV free. What came to my mind as Adam explained this is that when Jesus prayed for lepers he always sent them to the high priest to be examined and in the same way only the doctors could verify his sero-status. And therefore until he is certified he should still take medication, they told him. I also recall of how prophet Isaiah healed King Hezekiah even though God promised him 15 more years, the prophet gave Hezekiah medication and ointment to anoint his boil and treat his deadly condition until he was fully healed.

So contrary to beliefs that medication is aa show of doubt and faithlessness, we see the true folly of ignoring God's own ways of healing through doctors. Even Jesus avoided the folly of jumping off the temple in the naïve belief that the angels would indeed catch him. Misapplication of scripture, is a sure way of cutting short your life and destiny and in no way should we be gullible. Jesus was not, and neither should we.

Adam then explained that he bemoans the bad advice of pastors who tell people to stop ART treatment when the doctors have not certified them HIV free because this needlessly cuts short their lives and this folly would have equally cut short both his life and also God's purpose and the impact he would have had on many other people including you, the reader of his testimony. He said "Miraculously God healed my wife and she is HIV free and our child born in 2006 is also HIV free. It's God's grace on me that I pray for people even with cancer and they get healed instantly and doctors certify them healed but for me God has told me 'my grace is sufficient for you' so, just like Paul, this is my thorn in the flesh but I am satisfied that I have Jesus and I am serving God faithfully. You can take everything from me but just give me Jesus. I can walk in fire but if God is with me I am ok. Because he is the consuming fire. If you are in the fire with God you will not die. Just like Shadrach, Meshach and Abednego,, they were in the fire but were not consumed because they had the God who is a consuming fire and he has the power to consume the physical fire!

I preach mostly about the kingdom of more than mere Christianity because not all who are called Christians will enter the kingdom of God but only the saints, those who are truly born again'.

Adam is now a pastor and has a specific ministry to people living with HIV and Aids in addition to his commission of healing that continues to this day.

24

Olivia

The choirmaster who taught a new song

Olivia was a choirmaster for her local church and choir practice was every Saturday morning. Their choir would gather at the local primary school whose classes would always be open on the Saturday. After all, they had no use of the church during practice because, like most local choirs, they had no use of any instruments. It was a traditional church that did not actually frown on instruments, but tradition was so strong that their approach 'simply worked' as it had done for generations before. Also, they were in a rural area and were not really exposed to instruments in churches. Not that instruments did not exist, but they were a bit pricy and in such short supply that only 'bands' that were larger and more commercial, had them. So if it ain't broke why fix it right? And this wisdom remained true for them as it did for many choirs before them.

The weather was particularly sunny that Saturday morning and they would arrive one by one from 9 am. Despite the entrenched concept of 'Malawian time' it seemed the choir was quite 'English' in time keeping and they would all arrive in time. They had to, because they would first need to clean the desks and ensure they are in a clean environment.

The windows would not need opening since, as with many public schools.... they would not be there in the first place. They would be broken and just exist as bare frames. That's why the cleaning was so important since the dust would accumulate because of this free air flow. The dust would always settle in the class and they didn't want to have a sore throat and lose their voice... so the cleaning was their first duty.

Olivia was passionate about her role as the leader of the choir. To be a good leader you needed to have several things. Firstly, you must appreciate the importance of the role and to her, she did not take herself as a mere 'choirmaster', she thought of herself as a 'music director'.

She also looked at the importance of the choir in the process of worship. They lead and bring people closer to God, they preach and strengthen through song, bringing hope and encouragement. They declare praise for their God to the world, and they bring people closer to God through worship. This 'director' role was no mere role, and if taken seriously you had to be creative, deeply spiritual and dedicated.

It would mean making sure that the songs sang each Sunday are in line with the preaching and they don't distract or contradict the message of the day. This was such an important role to her, so much so that it often meant writing new songs that are fit for purpose. It also meant teaching new songs if these themed songs are already there in hymn books or were already sang by other musicians. So, this particular Saturday, she was in the mood for teaching them new songs.

Since hers was a 'ladies' choir, on this particular day she said, excitedly, of course,

'ladies we're learning new songs today, we'll have a little bit of the old but mostly mixed with the new. These are the songs you will sing tomorrow.'

Now, in group dynamics there is always an inquisitive one, so one of the ladies asked her 'we haven't sang new songs for a while so why, all of a sudden, are we learning new songs?'

'Just sing them. I am telling you…. these songs are going to be sang and have to be sang because they give a lot of hope and comfort'

They tried to winge and complain but Olivia insisted. And when Olivia insists, well, you know.

So they started their practice. They sang a few warm up melodies first, just to get their vocal cords open and in tune. Once their voices were going, Olivia started teaching the songs. Unfortunately, it was not just one, but several. Again they asked why they should sing these songs, and again Olivia was insistent 'you will sing all of them' she said, simply, authoritatively and unusually so.

So they continued, and continued. Now if you new Olivia she was not just any type of music director she was meticulous. That meant you can't do a half-baked job and you must give it your all if you're to be part of the choir. Anyone who would give a mediocre performance would get her immediate attention and guidance, needless to say, until things were 'just right'.

That day she almost got on people's nerves as the sense of perfection was quite high, and as time went along, the atmosphere changed and they got into the spirit. The sense of purpose for that day's practice was just over the roof, or perhaps 'over the chords' in a musical sense, and soon everyone sang with heart and soul. The songs were so captivating and they could sense an unusually strong presence of God's gracious spirit.

'Ladies, thank you for your dedication and passion today, may God richly bless you, but please remember the songs we sang today, you will sing them again to tomorrow, I will not be able to sing with you as I won't be there so please sing them well'.

The choir was happy following her encouragement and, since time had gone, did not bother to ask why she would not be able to sing tomorrow. The leader had spoken and they had to comply So they all went their separate ways and returned home.

Olivia came home and was quite jolly. She did her household tasks for that evening making sure the meals were done and everything was in order before going to bed. As she was about to retire she started feeling odd. A bit of a fever and a headache and she was getting weaker and weaker by the hour. She later started feeling body pains and felt sore in her joints. Soon she was having trouble breathing and was short of breath. Her breathing kept getting shallower and shallower, and shallower and shallower, until she could breathe no more. She died just like that, as if resting or sleeping when one wants to 'catch their breath'.

News of her passing soon spread like a wild fire as her death was announced in her community that very night. This type of announcement is quite traditional indeed, usually a bell boy, not a hotel bell boy, but a literal boy with a bell goes around the community ringing his bell and announcing, on top of his voice,

'Maliro! Maliro! ('ding dong' goes the bell).

Mai Olivia atisiya' ('ding dong' goes the bell)

In other words

'Funeral! Funeral! (Ding dong)

mama Olivia has passed on', (Ding dong)

It's a most effective way of spreading messages in a community when you don't have cell phones or those with phones are already sleeping and it works in both urban and rural settings, as it has centuries before.

The deputy choir director was shocked, as were all the choir members, to hear this devastating news.

'How could she die?' They said

'She was strong and healthy and we spoke with her just this afternoon! We had choir practice with her and she was teaching us new songs today'

Her funeral was held the next day and the same church choir was asked to sing the funeral songs. Soon the ladies said to themselves,

'Olivia knew she would not be here today, we just did not ask her why she would not be here but she said, 'I won't be here tomorrow to sing the songs with you but you must sing these songs'. So how can we sing anything else when we were given clear instructions to sing these songs?'

The decision was not just obvious but also unanimous. They had to sing Olivia's songs and that's exactly what they did. They were in pain and shock but they were also in a deep sense of strength and comfort as they sang stanza after stanza of these spirit inspired songs.

Tears were dropping and streaming down their cheeks but there was an aura about the funeral proceedings. There was a very strong presence of God. The presence was so strong that the peace of God filled people's hearts through the pain and shock. They knew Olivia was gone but they also knew she was in heaven. They knew that she knew where she was going and they knew she was ready to go home to heaven. Ready enough to insist, one last time, on what songs must be sang at her funeral to give hope and comfort. She was a real musical director who directed music even at her own funeral.

25

Chloe

The lady who pleaded to go home

Chloe was a pastor's wife and she was battling cancer for about two years now. Early in the week her condition had deteriorated and her husband Ted rushed her to hospital. Fortunately she stabilized and was discharged after an overnight admission. When Ted and Chloe arrived home that Wednesday Chloe said something strange,

'Honey, you need to release me and let me go, I have suffered so much these two years aren't you feeling sorry for me? My path has already been prepared and my door is already open. I too am ready. But it's your prayers that are holding me. Please honey you need to let me go'.

Ted looked at his sweetheart with such a curious look. He knew she was in so much pain and was heavily medicated so he felt sorry for her supposedly, delusional ramblings and hoped she would get better soon.

As Chloe rested and recuperated she took an unexpected turn for the worst on the Friday night and into the early hours of Saturday morning. Ted battled with the thought of taking her back to hospital, but Chloe said

'don't take me to hospital babe, you are just troubling me, I already told you that you're wasting your time by going to the hospital. My path is already set, and I can see it. I can also see that my door is already opened. And I can see where I am going. It's a beautiful place and my house is a beautiful house. You need to let me go because it's just your prayers that are holding me back. I have suffered enough these past two years and have been in so much pain please consider me in this and let me go so I am delivered from my pain.

These words were just too clear for Ted and it stopped him right in his tracks. He knew she needed care and planned to take her to hospital in the morning. contrary to her request and as a way of managing her expectations. So he decided to do something radical. He called Chloe's mom and sister, and said please come as soon as you can today. But since it was late in the evening and public transportation was a problem at this time they said

'we can't make it this evening we won't be able to travel. Can we make it tomorrow please?

'If it's tomorrow please come before 6 am so we can go to church but please, please, please, come through without fail!'

Early the next morning the two in-laws arrived at about 7 am due to delays in the public transport system.

Ted welcomed them into their home, exchanged niceties and then presented his issue,

'Mum, I am happy that you are well and thank you both for coming today, I have called you because of Chloe and her ailment. As you know she has been ill for a very long time now and this week she wasn't doing too well and we took her to hospital as you very well know. And yesterday she also took a turn for the worse. However, I called you because of the words she spoke to me on Wednesday and again yesterday as she refused to go back to hospital.

She told me that she has suffered for a long time and that she is ready to go but our prayers are holding her back. She also said her path is set and she can see her path to heaven and that her door is already open. She can also see where she is going and she says heaven is waiting for her.

Now when she told me these words the first time I did not

understand her. But when she repeated them yesterday I understood them differently and, as a pastor, I believe that she is speaking deep things. At first I thought she was not in her right mind but listening to her the second time I can see that she is in her right mind and that we need to consider her request as being genuine. Since she says it's our prayers that are holding her back and that she is ready to go, I think her request that we need to release her might be real. So what do you say on this matter mum?

'Apongozi, ("Son in law") I have heard what you have said and considering all you have said, Before I take her to hospital I thought you should know this development. I can see the need that we don't need to hold her back any longer. I know that she has suffered for a long time and I believe that what she is saying is true and that she is ready to meet her maker. I believe that she is going home. So it's ok I release her'

'Thank you Mum, and you sis? What do you say?'

'I agree with mom, I am also releasing her so she can go home, if her door is already open and her way home is ready, then there is no need for us to hold her back'

'Thank you sis. I too am releasing her. I have stayed with her and seen how much pain she has gone through, I don't want her to go through this when heaven is already open and ready to receive her. I also know her living faith in Jesus and that she really has a home in heaven. So Mum, please pray a short prayer to release her'

'Dear God, thank you for Chloe and the life and gift she was to us all. I release her into your gracious hands and pray that you receive and welcome her home. In Jesus name I pray, Amen'

'Thank you Mum. Sis please say a prayer for her release too'

'Dear God, thank you for Chloe, for such a blessing of a sister and such a close friend she was, thank you for her life. And now I release her into your hands that you will receive her. In Jesus name I pray, Amen'

'Thank you all very much, I too will say a prayer,

'Thank you father for my wife Chloe and the gift she was, I too release her into you hands and I thank you for her life and the blessing she has been to us all, Amen'

After these prayers were said, Ted thanked her mum and sister for coming, and explained that, as they had seen, the matter was such that he needed their urgency and their critical input and he was grateful for their prayers.

As he finished these niceties, hardly two minutes later, Chloe, sitting on the sofa took a deep breath and exhaled. As she exhaled she closed her eyes and breathed no more.

They all looked at her as she leaned her head as if in sleep. They touched her neck and felt no pulse, her wrists too and felt no pulse and she could not respond to the mention of her name. They all knew what had happened. Chloe had gone home and soon after she was released she took a deep breath and departed from this earth and her sickly body.

As the story comes to a close, one thing of note is the prayer by Ted on the day of the funeral. Before they lowered the coffin into the ground, Ted prayed a moving prayer

'Heavenly Father, thank you for giving me Chloe thank you forgiving me a soldier to fight along with in your army. I salute her and I know that she is already with you in heaven and that here we are just burying her body. But I salute her body for the soldier she was and the gift she was. Thank you for Chloe and her life and the blessing she was not just to me but to the body of Christ as a whole.

Father I pledge today that I will not stop fighting in the army of the Lord, I will preach the gospel and I will preach and serve you until the day I die! Amen and amen!'

As soon as he said 'amen', the crowd at the funeral, all together said a very deep and emphatic 'Amen!'

Chloe's story inspired many that she was more than ready to go home and that God had indeed prepared for her, a lovely home!

26

Secret Things

DANIELLE AND STACY

Stories perhaps never meant to be understood

DANIELLE

Sometimes stories seem completely unrelated and yet they teach us one and the same thing. In the previous stories we perhaps saw a divine intervention of sorts which comforted us of the passing of those we read about. But sometimes we don't have that privilege and there are many instances in which we can only wonder at what and why something has happened. But you know what?... Such things do happen and they happen a lot! Maybe these stores will speak to someone in that situation.

Danielle hadn't been feeling too well for a while now. She wasn't much of a doctor's person. Perhaps something she took after her mum, who normally had to be forced to seek any type of medical attention.

But this was something even she knew she needed medical attention for. So, though uncharacteristic of her, off she went to the doctor.

A series of tests were run and nothing showed as being amiss. A few weeks later however her symptoms returned and she again went to the doctor. This time her symptoms were more severe than before. She had further tests but nothing positive came up from her results.

Now, being the only girl in a family of 5 kids she was the princess of her family. Later on her family would rally around her, trying to help. Her mom, particularly, with whom she was so close, proved to be a strong pillar who always stood by her side. As they visited the doctors some gave one diagnosis and others gave another. Their diagnoses looked plausible but sometimes sounded contradictory and confusing. What was more apparent was the fact that the confusion led to being a disease in itself. Confusion led to despair and despair led to depression. Over time her response to medication was less than expected. Meanwhile her band of brothers, quite a loving and pious bunch, stood with her. Encouraging her to overcome her phobia of medication and keep to the treatments being given to her. The whole family in fact stood by her and all her brothers including her mum and Dad and her aunt Laura would all set aside days of prayer and fasting. Praying for her healing and God's intervention in her situation. Praying for clarity of her problem and wisdom to her doctors. One of her brothers, David, was in church one Sunday and received a prophecy which literally did not make sense to him and he simply brushed it off. But his wife at times would have nightmares of a dark cloud that had engulfed someone close to her.

Shortly after, a fresh round of tests finally revealed something. The doctors said unfortunately they missed something in the initial tests and the nature of her illness was such that it was easy to misdiagnose her, especially with the type of symptoms which were similar to other common diagnoses. Though some time had gone by, the doctors put her on the right treatment and everyone was relieved that at least there is more certainty and clarity now. At least their prayers were being answered.

As she started her new treatment, she was admitted to hospital for closer supervision. The doctors where hopeful but also told her family that her chances would have been better had the correct diagnosis been made sooner because this is not something that is difficult to treat in this day and age. David had travelled on work business but though he was out of country called Danielle to check on her as he did every day. She told him to buy him a beautiful dress. 'I want a dress' she said 'a long and beautiful and pure white dress.' 'Ok no worries sis I will do that.' He said.

However, shortly after that call her situation would deteriorate because she was not responding well to her medication. The doctors explained it was due to late diagnosis and that her chances were know 50:50. Late on Saturday night Danielle called her brother David and told him she was 'not feeling ok'. David prayed with her and encouraged her over the phone quoting scripture and telling her to be encouraged. After that call he knew something was up. She doesn't just call at 1 am.

Shortly after her call to David, Danielle talked to her mother and said 'mom can you see that bright white curtain?' 'No I don't see any-thing' her mom said. 'It's shiny and bright and beautiful and I see angels dressed in white... they are calling me to go there'.

Her mom knew what was going on and told her 'Don't go dear, don't go'.

Meanwhile David sensed something was going on and prayed during the night quoting scripture and praying in tongues until he had so much faith that Danielle would get better. Something he specifically prayed for over and over again that night was that God would send angels to minister to her. He didn't know what was going on in hospital and this 'white curtain' experience was only told to him a few days later. For some reason he could not stop praying about this.... 'I pray for your angels to minister to her, your angels to surround her, your angels to bear her so she may not dash her foot against a stone, I pray for powerful and angelic ministration over her right now.' So he prayed and prayed.

By the time he finished praying, it was now 5 am. He had literally prayed through the night! After this prayer, David had a great sense of assurance that everything would be ok. His heart was extremely calm as if there was no crisis. He could not explain it. He believed for the best but somehow he was audaciously calm, so calm he could not understand why.

However, being in different cities he and his wider family started traveling from their different cities to go and visit her again. Most of them making another of several trips now religiously made at each weekend to check on her. By the time he arrived at the hospital 320km away she had stopped talking.

She was under a lot of sedation and could barely overcome the strength of her medication. However, somehow she mustered some strength to raise her right hand as in a waving fashion but it would come down shortly after. David and everyone else prayed for her on her bedside and encouraged her, talking to her even though she couldn't talk back, and left for home.

At 4 am the next day phones started ringing in her brothers' homes. Danielle had passed on! At least that's what the phone calls said.

They all rushed to the hospital and found the doctors trying as hard as they could to resuscitate her. David stood opposite Danielle's bed in her hospital room as if standing guard against an unseen enemy. He watched, painfully so, as they tried all sorts of things. Later, his presence was noticed and they asked him to leave the room so they could continue to provide the necessary help. But alas, merely a few minutes later he sensed silence in the room and instead of the sounds of doctors trying to help her. Nurses rushed out of the room wheeling her bed out of the ward with a sheet over her body. It was obvious what had happened.

The family started funeral arrangements and burial was in the days shortly after. David being the first born brother had a big weight on his shoulders but what could he do? It was his first funeral to organize but an important one..... He didn't know what to do but did what he could until all arrangements were made and his sister was successfully laid to rest. But during this three day ordeal, as grueling as it was, he had the same sense of calm he felt when he had prayed for his little sister. Then it hit him!

He got a prophecy in church a month before the funeral which said that 'you are like Joseph of Aramathea who was given the task of burying the Lord Jesus'. At the time it meant nothing to him and instead of cracking his head trying to decipher the prophecy he simply resigned to the fact that it would make sense in time if, at all, it is anything to go by. Could this mean what he thought it meant? Did this mean that God knew even though they stood by her that Danielle's time had come? And that he would in-fact be given the task of burying his sister? After all that prayer and all that fasting? And that, not only by him but his whole family? And what of the hand she was constantly waving when she could not speak? Was she actually waving goodbye when we thought she was simply weak? What of the white dress she wanted? The long white dress? It would serve as a reminder that she never got a chance to wear it... but wait! Could it be she was admiring a dress code of the saints she saw beyond the curtain? He remained in wonder... The only solace he had was the vision of beauty and light Danielle saw behind the curtain! and her being beckoned home...

STACY

In a totally unrelated story to Danielle's, Robin was a devout Christian He was a church secretary and so instrumental in the church administration. He was what you would consider a pillar of the church, and had a lovely energetic daughter named Stacy.

Stacy was an intelligent young lady. Now in college and dreaming big in life. One weekend she and her friends went out for some drinks and her mom expected her home soon since she rarely stayed out very late. For some reason Robin fell asleep early and didn't hear Stacy go out that night. His wife, Emma, had prepared breakfast and put the cereals and pancakes out for Stacy to eat once she wakes up. Shortly after she wondered at the silence in Stacy's room. "She must have overslept" she said to herself "let her rest". A while later she came to her bedroom door and knocked loud enough for Stacy to hear.

'Breakfast is ready pumpkin' she said but there was silence.

Stacy, now a big girl, actually, a young lady, hated the term. She now felt of age and that she had outgrown the term "pumpkin". But Smart as mothers are, that's exactly the term she used when to irritate her and ensure she wakes up, even in her sleep she would mumble, "mum I'm a big girl, I'm not your pumpkin anymore".

'But you will always be my little pumpkin dear, no matter how old you are" she would answer. And whenever she called "Stacy dear", she would continue sleeping.

If there is nothing immediate she would let her sleep in, but when there is something urgent she would always call her "pumpkin" ... and that would do the trick, always.

She called again opened the door and saw an empty bed.

'Oh' she thought to herself 'that's odd!' She was unsure of what to feel... anger that she did not come home or concern to know where she is? As a mother her concern overpowered her anger as her motherly instinct kicked in. She reached for her phone and dialed Stacy's number. The call however could not get through and all she could hear on the other line was, 'The called party cannot he reached'.

She tried to call repeatedly with no success. The more she tried the more anxious she got! And she started getting cold shivers down her spine. Something is not right she said. She ran to Robin and told him about Stacy's disappearance. It was now mid-morning getting into lunch time and still there was no sign of Stacy. They started making phone calls to Stacy's friends. They all explained that they were together but she left with some other friends and did not come back. They called their family friends and relations in close proximity asking if their Stacy had shown up in their homes but all to no avail. They hurried themselves to the police station as soon as they could but were met with the usual protocol.

'How old is the daughter Sir?

How long has she been missing?

Who was she with and when was she last seen?' Asked the policeman to which Robin replied and explained everything.

The officer took off his glasses, looked Robin in the eye and said

'Well sir it's not yet 24 hours after her disappearance so we can only open an investigation after 24 hour's. Besides it's a girl sir, girls don't go missing'

'What does that mean' he said, now translated in his vernacular language it reads 'atsikana samasowa' a common saying in their culture that girls are the attraction of men so she's probably having fun and enjoying herself somewhere. It's a little vulgar and offensive and does not assume the best of morals. So Robin fumed in anger!

'My little angel is not that'

'Oh I'm sorry sir, I did not mean to offend you sir, but please wait for your daughter and if she doesn't come back please let us know so we open a missing person's case'.

He pleaded with the officer to open a case immediately, but they had to follow protocol! He then went again in the evening and told that now its 24 hours and his daughter is still nowhere to be seen. The police opened a case file and asked a few more questions, gathering all necessary information for their investigation.

He went home and sat with his wife on the dining chair eyes fixed to the door and then frequently peeking at the window, waiting for their daughter's return instinctively and after the the sound of very passing car.

But, hours would turn into days and days would turn into weeks and this remained their routine, waiting by the door, calling her number and never getting through. With every passing hour and every passing day a piece of her seemed to slip away as their anguish grew with every chime of their clock. During this time, their church stood by them. Praying and fasting that God would do a miracle. The Men's group to which Robin belonged came by and prayed and talked with them.

One Saturday afternoon Robin heard a knock at the door. His heart skipped a beat and running to the door he opened it quickly. Perhaps it's my baby girl he thought! But behind the door was a man in police uniform.

"Is this the home of Mr. Daniels?

Yes sir it is

Mr. Robin Daniels?" He asked again.

"Yes"

he replied. At this the police man took off his hat and held it close to his chest.

'I am sorry sir, but I need you to come with me to the hospital'

'What for?'

'It's best you just come sir, it's to do with the disappearance of your daughter'

'Is she okay is she receiving treatment in hospital?'

Now looking him straight in the eye

'No sir I'm sorry sir, we need to go to the hospital morgue and need you you to identify a body sir. We think it fits the description of your daughter but we're not sure sir'

This was not the news they were hoping for, but at this point any news was better that no news. He quickly told his wife and they hurriedly went to the morgue. The policeman told them that since they were not certain they should be prepared for the possibility that it's not their daughter. But they thought it's important for them to assist them in their investigation.

He prepared them by telling them it's not a very pleasant sight so they should brace themselves. Emma and Robin took a deep breath as the morgue personnel opened the body bag. Immediately a pungent stench filled the room. The body they saw was barely whole. It seemed to have been mutilated with no eyes, ears and lips. They could not recognize who this person was but wait the blouse! And the dress, and finally the shoes. All of these belonged to their baby girl. The police man explained that other parts of her body had been mutilated and it looked like this was a ritual killing for superstitious practices that had gone rampant in the area.

Then they saw a birthmark on her chest which confirmed to them their fears. Their hearts sank at the realization that the one before them was indeed their baby girl. They were astounded at how this could happen when they faithfully served God in their church. When the whole church had stood by them. When the church Pastor had constantly prayed with them and encouraged them. When the Men's church fellowship had fasted with them. When they themselves had constantly prayed and fasted. Of all deaths and of all people why a ritual killing and why their baby girl?

They searched their hearts and wondered if perhaps they had done something wrong and if this was God's punishment? Was it because of the tithe they missed to pay due to the school fees they paid for their daughter and was God saying "even though you are spending on her you ought to have spent it on me?" Or was it the pledge offering he forgot to fulfill? Could it be he was praying a miss or did not pray enough? Whatever it was he cried at God's feet and asked for forgiveness and enlightenment to avoid this in future.

Fortunately, Robin and Emma had a strong support system, as family and relatives rallied around them for the funeral. And the church, oh the church played a key role of comforting them as a family. Exactly 2 months after the funeral there was a men's fellowship meeting and it was testimony time. As people gave their testimonies everyone was energized at the great works God was doing in their lives. Then Robin raised his hand to give a testimony and the hall went deathly quiet,.. as he walked to the front everyone wondered at what he would say considering their recent family ordeal. But then he started to talk,

"I know you must all be wondering about what I want to say. The last few months I and my wife Emma have gone through so much pain and trauma and many of you could not even talk to us because you did not know what to say. I know that you cared but were unable to reach out to us. When our daughter died we were filled with every imaginable emotion you could think of... We were angry, confused and most of all simply in anguish because of our ordeal.

But one day when I was praying to God and asking him why this had to happened to us God spoke to me. He said "who does Stacy's life belong to? Did you create her life? And when I gave her to you did she stop being mine?

I gave you a gift for a short while but she was with you for safe-keeping only. When the time came for me to take her I only took what was mine! So don't ask me why I took her because I am only taking what is mine?"

When God spoke to me in this way I realized that God is sovereign and I cannot put him on the judgment stand. I realized that God owns everything and he does not really owe me an explanation. I realized that though this was a tragedy he allowed it to happen and all he did was call back what already belongs to him. My daughter is gone but I can only commit her to God's hands and I know that in spite of our ordeal God is in control. That is the peace I have. It gave me freedom to know that God is not condemning or judging me for my sins and shortfalls because they are covered by the blood of Jesus. And God is in control. This gives me great peace!"

When Robin gave his testimony, the gathering finally got encouragement and a great sense of peace. They were relieved that God himself was comforting Robin and Emma, even in ways that they themselves could not.

So here we have two unrelated stories, but what is related about them is that in all stories the expectations of good and godly people were not fulfilled. Also, in both stories, God was not overwhelmed with the situation. God was still in control.

No matter how painful, gruesome and devastating the loss seems to be, God is still on his throne and God is in control. God is never taken by surprise! Whatever trauma and pain you may be experiencing you can still trust this fact.... "God is in control!"

27

What People Are Saying...

"I couldn't put the book down"

"Reading this book is like watching a movie"

'After many months of procrastinating, I finally read the book...I've personally been challenged by the different stories, to do more and live with a consciousness that life is short"

"I felt so much peace and joy at the thought of heaven... Thank you for saying yes to God and publishing this book!'

'Thank you for writing that book, I don't know what I would have done now without it... I thought I was reading it to heal my previous loss, but it was prophetic and prepared me for my Dad's passing, my little kids are also reading it and it's giving them closure for the loss of their dad'

'This book has changed the way I look at life, and how I relate to God! You are no longer the same after reading it'

"Three weeks ago I lost a sibling, yesterday I lost an uncle, God has been good to me through your spirit inspired words in this book, I believe that what God has done to me he can also do to my family through your books"

"I lost my Dad when I was 15 and only now, after reading your book twenty years later do I have closure! Thank you Moffat."

28

The Door to Heaven

A prayer for those who want to make heaven their home

Dear Jesus, you have said that "I am the way, the truth and the life". Today I choose to believe that indeed you are the way to heaven, and the way to my heavenly father, you are the truth of the world and you are my life!

I believe you have gone to heaven to prepare a place for me to prepare room for me in your father's house You have said "there are many rooms in my father's house" and "where I am going you will be also." Jesus I want to go to heaven I want to come home after this life I want to come to my father in heaven! Therefore I ask for the forgiveness of my sins through The shed blood of Jesus as the only atonement for my sin I confess with my mouth that Jesus you are the Lord of my life and I receive you as my personal savior

I believe that you rose again from the dead, I thank you that you have forgiven my sin and written my name in the book of life

In Jesus name I have prayed... Amen

Name ....   Date ....